TURNING THE TIDE IN THE WEST

**An urgent call
for church revival
and spiritual awakening
in today's world**

Desmond E. Daniels

All Scripture quotations, unless otherwise indicated, are taken from the Holy Bible, New King James Version®. Copyright © 1982 by Thomas Nelson. Used by permission. All rights reserved.

Scripture quotations marked (NIV) are taken from the Holy Bible, New International Version®, NIV®. Copyright © 1973, 1978, 1984, 2011 by Biblica, Inc.™ Used by permission of Zondervan. All rights reserved worldwide. www.zondervan.comThe "NIV" and "New International Version" are trademarks registered in the United States Patent and Trademark Office by Biblica, Inc.™

Scripture quotations marked (NLT) are taken from the Holy Bible, New Living Translation, copyright © 1996. Used by permission by Tyndale House Publishers, Inc., Wheaton Illinois 60189. All rights reserved.

Copyright 2022 © Desmond E. Daniels. All rights reserved

ISBN: 978-0-6453238-1-8

Printed in Australia
by Creative Visions Print & Design
www.cvpd.com.au

Acknowledgments

I am indebted to my Lord and Savior Jesus Christ, who alone can turn the tide in these days and without whose help I would not have written this book. His love and faithfulness to every generation have given me the confidence to seek and expect revival in these troubled times.

Special thanks to my wife and best friend, Pauline; without her help and support, I could not have written this book.

Additionally, I would like to express my appreciation to our children David, Libby, and Bec, together with their spouses, who have prayed and supported me throughout this journey.

This whole project was birthed in prayer and supported by many faithful prayer partners along the way. I want to thank Neil and Dolores De Haan and Everton and Tulia Edwards on the East Coast of the United States, together with Pastor Oden Fong and his online prayer warriors on the West Coast, for their prayers. My friend Chip Cimino also on the U.S. West Coast has also been a faithful prayer warrior for myself personally as well as this writing project.

I thank Alan Hood for his helpful feedback and encouragement: and John Bryant for his invaluable assistance in editing and publishing this book. Finally, I want to thank Joshua Mayne for his invaluable help building my website, www.desdaniels.com

About the Author

Des Daniels was a Baptist minister in Sydney, Australia. After completing ministry studies at Morling College, he pastored a number of churches and during his first visit to the USA in the 1980s he saw the Jesus Movement first-hand. This experience, together with the study of history's great awakenings, gave him a burden for prayer & revival in these days. As he was writing this book Des was diagnosed with a sarcoma which led to an incredible health journey lasting 3 years. He went home to be with Jesus in December 2022.

What Others are Saying about this Book

In this book, Des has shared his Spirit-inspired passion for the renewal of Western Christianity through honest, God-driven revival. He takes us on a journey through the wastelands of modern philosophical directions and leads us to the point where we are left in no doubt that the world's future depends on our return to honest and Scripturally based faith. The examples of previous revivals and works of the Spirit whet our appetites for a new, world-changing movement of God based on love, truth, and godly obedience. This book is easy to read and understand and is impossible to put down once started. But be warned, God speaks through this book, and your name may well be on God's lips!

Alan R. Hood,
Lead Pastor
Rouse Hill Baptist Church
Sydney, Australia

I read Des Daniels' book while contemplating the massive decline in Australian churchgoing in recent years. Fifty years ago, 36% of the Australian population attended a Christian church at least monthly; today, it's just 15%. So numerically, some 5 million people have voted with their feet! Couple that with society's mania for materialism and our plummeting moral standards, and we have a toxic cocktail. However, Des's well-researched book unexpectedly offers the ultimate solution, supported by solid Biblical and contemporary evidence. He doesn't suggest a new political party or economic system but rather a route as old as the one through the Red Sea. Every rank-and-file Christian believer can play a pivotal role in becoming part of a proven solution. And it's the simplicity of his proposal that encourages me that Des has nailed it!

John Bryant
Greater West for Christ
New Church Paradigm Team
Sydney, Australia

What Others are Saying about this Book

I have known Des Daniels for several decades, both as a good friend and as a dedicated, no-nonsense, loving pastor. Several years back, God strongly impacted Des concerning the great need for revival in the church. The communication between God and Des was remarkable; not unlike God calling the prophet Jeremiah and Jeremiah's response that he was not qualified for the task. Des spent the first year solely in fervent prayer for revival. During this prayer time, he received the inspiration to write a book. Every word, sentence, and paragraph were carefully selected while seeking divine guidance as to what to say to the reader. The fruit of Des' labor is within these pages, under God's inspiration.

Oden Fong
Senior Pastor
Poiema Christian Fellowship
Costa Mesa, California

I have had the privilege to journey with this God-burdened brother Des as he has battled and toiled to obediently speak out the Word of the LORD for the Western Church today. It boils down to God's unchanging Word in Scripture found in 2 Chronicles 7:14 to truly repent and abandon oneself to the incomparable life of holiness in Christ alone! Many church leaders have spoken of the need for revival and awakening in these times. This book takes us a step further to explain the spiritual principles involved and offers a way forward so that revival in our day becomes a real possibility.

Patrick Barker
Pastor
Tiverton Baptist Church
Tiverton, Devon, England

CONTENTS

Introduction The game has radically changed..........9

Part One: The West's Christian Foundations

Chapter One   The greatest reset in history..........15
Chapter Two   Heaven's peace plan..........31

Part Two: The spiritual tide in the west is out

Chapter Three   The need for revival today..........45

Part Three: Turning the tide

Chapter Four   The light is still shining 65
Chapter Five   The awakenings of the past..........77
Chapter Six   Re-digging the ancient wells..........89
Chapter Seven   Calling on the name of the lord..........101
Chapter Eight   The biblical pattern of awakening..........115
Chapter Nine   The church that jesus built 129
Chapter Ten   Making the main thing the *main* thing..........143

Epilogue 159

Endnotes 163

Introduction

THE GAME HAS RADICALLY CHANGED

> Liberty cannot be established without morality,
> nor morality without faith.
> Alexis de Tocqueville (1805-1859)
> *Democracy in America*

The ebb and flow of history

For the past 2,000 years, the West has experienced an ebb and flow of spiritual life that has impacted the growth and development of Western civilization. At present, the spiritual tide is well and truly out. Following the pattern of history, this has resulted in both a moral and spiritual malaise.

The Dark Ages was one of the better-known spiritual ebbs when the light and life of the Gospel was replaced by superstition and empty religious observance. However, as well as these ebbs, there have also been flows when the tide turned, bringing revival in the church and spiritual awakening in the society. Darkness creates and generates a need for the light, which is why these revivals and awakenings occurred at some of history's darkest times. People turning to the light enjoy individual faith and create an impetus for spiritual progress and social advancement. While the blows being dealt by the Enlightenment, the French Revolution, and related movements were threatening the very existence of Christianity; here and there less spectacular developments were indications of a fresh tide of life which was to make that religion more potent in mankind as a whole than ever before.[1] K.S. Latourette (1884-1968)

For several generations, the West was seduced by the man-made idol of secularism and the embrace of empty dead-end materialism. By contrast, the rest of the world is still open to spiritual reality, and the Gospel is being embraced by people who were previously closed to its truth. Secularism has proved popular in the West, promising all the benefits of the Gospel without the moral price tag. It has sought to address the human aspiration for a better world but has not delivered its promised utopias. Being man-made, it contains no life, and just like all the other idols in history, it cannot save man from himself. Because of this, the West is now experiencing a spiritual and moral malaise that no amount of tweaking can remedy. Its only hope is in the turning of the spiritual tide and returning to its traditional foundations.

The turning of the tide always flows from a pent-up desire for something more satisfying, better, and higher. In turn, this creates a protest against the chaos, confusion, and frustration that godlessness always produces. This is why I firmly believe we are beginning to see another turning of the tide in the West. Several indicators suggest that we will experience a revival in the Church and spiritual awakening in the West in these days:

- The evident spiritual hunger in society
- The lack of a spiritual roadmap and moral compass in the West
- The way God has worked in the past gives hope for a movement in the future
- The unfulfilled promises of a future time of advancement of the Gospel
- God's promises to answer the prayers of His people

The western malaise

It is no secret that Western civilization is currently displaying symptoms of a serious malaise for which there appears to be no human remedy. A malaise is defined as a general feeling of illness whose exact cause is unknown or difficult to diagnose. This sums up the condition of those living in the West when, despite unprecedented levels of democratic freedom and affluence, people appear to be increasingly unhappy. Instead of being the shining city upon a hill whose light is a beacon that guides freedom-loving people everywhere, the Western malaise has resulted in the questioning of even the viability of Western liberal democracy.

So, why have things gone so terribly wrong?

Like the prodigal son in Jesus' timeless parable, the West has left its traditional home, dazzled by the bright lights of a better future in the far country. Having left behind its traditional spiritual, moral, and cultural roots, it has squandered its Christian heritage on a delusory quest for a utopian society independent of God.

As with the son in Jesus' parable, the West's infatuation with secularism has fallen far short of people's expectations. Instead of the promised utopia, our culture is descending into a chasm of disappointment; life no longer satisfies the human soul. We could well label this outcome 'dystopia', which is the opposite of utopia. It is the state where no one is satisfied, and just about everything that could go wrong does. Our increasingly dystopian societies are characterized by cataclysmic decline, leaving people frustrated, unfulfilled, living increasingly dehumanized lives.

As our culture descends into dystopia, the age of reason has now become the age of post-modern, post-truth, and confusion. Despite its aspiration for a new age of peace and love, the West has grown less civil, more hostile, dangerously divided, and deeply conflicted. Putting things as plainly as I possibly can, the cultural revolution against the Christian foundations of the West hasn't worked. The results don't align with the claims made by the high priests of the Secularist Religion. Their faith and trust in the ability of man to redeem himself apart from God were sadly misplaced.

Their faith and trust in the ability of man to redeem himself apart from God were sadly misplaced.

We must remember, however, that in the pendulum swing of history, Western civilization has been here before. There have been other times in our history when the spiritual tide was well and truly out, and it looked as though the light of the Gospel would be extinguished. For example, before the *First Great Awakening*, Voltaire predicted that Christianity would be forgotten in 30 years. This intellectually brilliant, although spiritually blind man, was not counting on what God was going to do. Beginning with the coming of Jesus, there have been several times throughout history—often in the darkest of times, when the tide turned. In response to the prayers of His people, God stepped down into the affairs of men to fulfill His plans and purposes.

This is what we are hoping for today.

In the following pages, we are going to be reminded that the time for cursing the darkness has passed, and the need of the hour is a widespread turning back to the light. The spiritual, cultural and psychological malaise that I will be describing more fully in a later chapter is no mere accident. Rather it is the inevitable outcome of a civilization and culture that has rejected its foundations and the things that gave it life, health, and well-being.

As well as describing some of the impacts of past awakenings, we will also consider some of the spiritual principles that can help us in our quest to turn the tide of godlessness in our generation.

Every news update of every day illustrates the problems confronting us for which there are no human solutions. When we recognize this, the next step becomes a no-brainer! That is, we must turn back to God and seek *His* help. This is where revival and awakening begin because when people turn to God, everything changes. It is *then* that He steps down and moves in new ways.

PART ONE

THE WEST'S CHRISTIAN FOUNDATIONS

One

THE GREATEST RESET IN HISTORY

> The fall of the first man was a great revolution:
> the restoration of man by Jesus Christ
> was a counter-revolution.
> J.H. Merle d'Aubigne (1794-1872)[2]

The coming of Jesus changed our world forever. The Gospel's impact was such that even those who vehemently opposed its message complained that it had begun to turn the world upside-down (Acts 17:6)—or right-side-up depending on your perspective. The dictionary definition of a revolution is 'a sudden, radical, or complete change;'— that describes precisely the impact of the coming of Jesus. However, the Gospel's power wasn't that of political or military force but rather the effect of God's love on the hearts of men. Because of this, the divine love of God manifested in Jesus Christ became a beacon of hope that resonated in human hearts to bring people home to God.

Unlike the many human revolutions down through the centuries, Jesus' message was focused on bringing peace, not armed insurrection, to planet earth. When the apostle Peter took up a sword in a futile attempt to defend Jesus, he received a stern rebuke from his Master, who said, "Put your sword in its place, for all who take the sword will perish by the sword" (Matthew 26:52). Jesus' words were prophetically accurate of the French Revolution that sought to improve people's lives but instead created a bloodbath and a reign of terror. So too, the various manifestations of Marxism have been responsible for the deaths of an estimated 100 million people. By contrast, Heaven's Peace Plan that we will examine more closely in the next chapter, is designed as a roadmap to remove conflict and enable people to live together in peace and harmony.

The whole focus of Jesus' message was to show people the way home to God that is foundational to living life as God intended and being fully human. This was what changed everything. Jesus' parable of the Prodigal Son teaches the timeless and eternal truth that it was the heart-realization of what the prodigal had squandered and lost that led him home to his father. His abject poverty caused him to remember his heritage, roots, and true identity. He had left home believing that he knew more than his father, but it was the life lesson of failure that enabled him to value those things he had left behind. It was only after he had squandered his inheritance that his delusions were exposed and he 'came to himself.'

Western culture and civilization will need to recall its lost inheritance and treasure before returning home to its Christian roots. To reject Jesus is also to deny the blessings that He alone can bring—and especially the divine love that Jesus both taught and demonstrated. Heaven's gift to planet earth was and is Jesus Christ, the Son of God.

Although imperfectly implemented so far, the Christian faith provides the only roadmap for people on earth to live together in harmony, civility, and love. The teachings of Jesus alone provide the necessary balance between inner freedom and aspiration while also maintaining the moral imperative of love for others. Jesus taught and demonstrated that personal liberty could and must be balanced by a concern for the welfare of others and the seeking of the common good. The Gospel of Jesus alone has provided the unique form/freedom balance that has allowed Western civilization to grow and flourish. Jesus came to show the way to peace on earth that can only happen when people are at peace with themselves. He alone showed the way for people to overcome the restraints and limitations of their base humanity to attain a higher existence than people ever thought possible.

> Although imperfectly implemented so far, the Christian faith provides the only roadmap for people on earth to live together in harmony, civility, and love.

Before there can be a credible alternative to the darkness and confusion of the present day, there must first be an understanding—both outside and inside the Church, of the tremendous impact of the Gospel revolution that occurred 2000 years ago. The coming of Jesus ignited a fire of holy love that is still the most extraordinary power in the universe. The reason for its tremendous impact was that it found a ready response in human hearts that were already hardwired to receive and understand its message.

When we understand the universal need of our humanity to love and be loved, we will see that the Gospel is now more relevant than ever. In a conflicted and divided society that is, for the most part, motivated and ruled by selfishness, the Gospel is still transformative and incendiary. It still has the power to transform and elevate the human condition.

The Savior is born

The greatest revolution in history was birthed in the heart of God before the world was created and burst forth onto the earthly stage with an angelic announcement. The Savior of the world was born in Bethlehem of Judea. The light from heaven shone forth and the world would never be the same again.

> But the angel reassured them. "Don't be afraid!" he said. "I bring you good news of great joy for everyone! The Savior—yes, the Messiah, the Lord—has been born tonight in Bethlehem, the city of David! Luke 2:10-11 (NLT)

This angelic announcement of the Savior's birth was not made to the political, religious, or cultural elites of that day but to a group of humble shepherds who were dutifully tending their flocks at night. King Herod and his political cronies felt threatened by Jesus' birth. They actively worked to quench the flame of protest that Jesus' birth was about to ignite, and to extinguish the light of the world. By contrast, the humble shepherds responded to the message by dropping everything to run to Bethlehem to see the Savior for themselves. Having found the baby wrapped in swaddling clothes and lying in a manger—just as the angel had said, the shepherds returned to their duties 'glorifying and praising God' for what they had seen. God had stepped down into history to impact their lives and save the human race, and these humble shepherds were the first in a long line of believers who recognized Jesus for who He was: the Savior of the world.

The only way we can explain the birth and growth of the early Church is to understand the dynamic spiritual power that Jesus' teaching unleashed. As the apostle Paul later said, 'I am not ashamed of the Gospel of Christ, for it is the power of God to salvation for everyone who believes' (Romans 1:16). The Gospel of Jesus ignites an inner transformation that turns men's hearts from selfishness to love, from unbelief to faith, and from being confined by their selfish fallen nature to being filled with the Holy Spirit. What we call revival or awakening is simply a protest against the same-old, same-old, and a return to the power and purity of the New Testament standard of radical faith and devotion to God.

The Gospel of Jesus ignites an inner transformation that turns men's hearts from selfishness to love, from unbelief to faith, and from being confined by their selfish fallen nature to being filled with the Holy Spirit.

The light of the world has come

In Bethlehem, Judaea, the birth of Jesus impacted our planet more than anything before or since. In the coming of Jesus, God stepped into history, and a light from heaven shone into the darkness of planet earth to change and transform it forever. Jesus' coming had such a profound impact that today, all of history is divided into B.C., *before Christ* and A.D., Anno Domini, or *the years since Jesus came*. When this same light shines out in the present-day darkness and confusion, a new reset and turning to Jesus will be inevitable.

> Then Jesus spoke to them again, saying, "I am the light of the world. He who follows Me shall not walk in darkness, but have the light of life." John 8:12

The transformation ignited by the Gospel gave a wholly different worldview that completely transformed our understanding of everything. As well as providing the world insight into the laws of the universe that facilitated scientific discovery, the Christian worldview also gave purpose and meaning to our human existence. Supremely, however, it was about setting the whole human race free from those things that had held it back throughout history. Jesus came to remedy our fallen humanity that at its heart is motivated by selfish sinfulness by replacing it with an even stronger incentive; that is the power of divine love.

To fully understand the profound impact of the first Gospel revolution and its relevance today, we must first understand the darkness and confusion into which the Light of the World was to shine. The first-century Roman world was intellectually astute, politically sophisticated, and technologically advanced. However, it was also a cruel world governed by Caesar, who believed himself to be a god. This dark paganism of the Roman world was an expression of the darker side of base humanity with its will to pleasure and lust for power. This pagan worldview of gods and demigods rested on the belief that might-makes-right, eliminating individual rights and freedoms. Rome's political and military might showed no concern for the human aspirations for freedom, love, and peace that lay in the hearts of the people they conquered. It was into this world of pagan darkness that the light of the Gospel was to shine.

The truth of the Gospel and the Christian worldview was so far superior to anything previously known that it profoundly impacted what ultimately developed as the cradle of Western civilization. The Gospel revolution was of such epic proportions that within a generation, churches flourished in most of the large population centers of the Mediterranean world; the Gospel even penetrated the very palace of Caesar itself (Philippians 4:22).

> The impact was such that even the Roman Emperor bowed his knee to the humble Galilean. Within a few generations, Christianity became the official religion of the Empire, enabling it to develop, grow and flourish for nearly 2,000 years.

Jesus came to planet earth to shine the light of heaven into the darkness and confusion of a world that was both blind and deluded. It is no wonder that the angels rejoiced when Jesus was born because at long last, light, love and truth had come into this crazy dark world, and the Savior of the world had finally come. In a world that struggled to make sense of everything, Jesus came to provide a way of salvation and show us the way home to God. Supremely, He showed how to heal the selfish sinfulness that has made man his own worst enemy. Only then can we fulfill those aspirations vital to our humanity and embedded in our DNA. The Gospel's effect was to elevate people from the downward spiral that paganism always produces and lift society to a higher plane.

> And suddenly there was with the angel a multitude of the heavenly host praising God and saying: "Glory to God in the highest, And on earth peace, goodwill toward men!" Luke 2:13-14

Jesus came at just the right time

The apostle Paul, who was uniquely equipped and prepared by God to take the Gospel from the Middle East into Europe, recognized that Jesus was born at just the right time.[4] Jesus was the answer to man's long search for truth and meaning. He arrived on the scene when people everywhere were searching for answers.

Having been created in God's image, man is the only species on our planet that demands explanations for his existence. Pet-lovers understand that all a dog needs for ecstatic happiness and fulfillment is food, companionship, and an occasional walk! Humans, on the other hand, are a little more complicated. It is a part of our humanity that we feel incomplete without a sense of meaning and purpose. God has hardwired a spiritual appetite and a quest for eternity deep into our human nature. Throughout history, every nation and ethnic group has practiced religious expression—something in our humanity always aspires to something more and something higher.

When the good news of Jesus Christ was proclaimed to the Roman Empire of the 1st Century, it satisfied an inner longing – a spiritual hunger and thirst for God. In a real sense, finding Jesus was like coming home. For centuries, philosophers and theologians from the ancient world had pondered the meaning of life. They had wrestled with their mortality and sought to overcome the constrictions of death by seeking immortality in their various religions. The Egyptians, for example, sought to extend the existence of their Pharaohs by building pyramids to preserve their bodies and provide food for their afterlife.

> Something in their humanity protested the idea that death is final, and they instinctively yearned for and sought for immortality.

The ancient philosophers followed the simple logic that there had to be a designer and first cause in a universe with clear evidence of design. Therefore, this world couldn't have just happened. And so, the belief grew amongst the ancient Egyptian, Persian and Indian civilizations that behind this material world was *something more* and that this something, whatever it was, governed the universe . The Greek philosophers took this idea further and called this something the Logos; that is, the divine reason behind the universe.

> 'Logos'. In Greek philosophy and theology, the divine reason implicit in the cosmos, ordering it and giving it form and meaning. Encyclopedia Britannica.[6]

Jesus was born into this ancient world where there were more questions than answers, and His followers made the bold declaration that the logos they had been seeking had come to planet earth in the form of a man. Likewise, the First Century Church declared that the word or logos had been made flesh. Jesus Christ was the Creator God who had stepped down into history and visited this planet. The evidence supporting His claim was compelling, and His coming produced a protest against the prevalent spiritual and moral darkness of their age.

Not only did Jesus appear at just the right time—Jesus was also born in just the right place!

> The land where Jesus was born lies at the intersection of three continents and the confluence of three different cultures, each of which left its imprint on world history

The *Greek* culture left its imprint on the world through its intellectual prowess and philosophy. The New Testament was written in the vernacular (common) Greek language.

Jesus was also born in a country under *Roman* occupation that left its imprint on the world. The Romans had established an empire through military might, technological superiority, and advanced law and government. The Roman contribution to world history was profound. When Jesus was born, Caesar Augustus ordered his parents to travel to Bethlehem for a Roman census to facilitate more efficient taxation. Jesus was also a Jew, and Judaism's influence permeated the world into which He was born. Jesus could trace his family tree through King David back to Abraham, and the Jewish religion, with its Law and Temple worship, has left an indelible mark on our world.

Each of these three cultures represented the highest human attainments in the fields of philosophy, government, and religion. However, each was destined to be surpassed by the teachings of Jesus in light of the Gospel.

> The City of God is built at the confluence of three civilizations.
> Conybeare and Howson[7]

As high as these human attainments had been, they paled into insignificance compared to the truth and power they encountered with the Gospel of Jesus. No force on earth could stop the good news from spreading throughout the Roman Empire. The news spread that Jesus had conquered death and risen from the grave. This earth-shattering message could not be ignored, then—or now. Any student of history will see that the spread of the Christian Church in its earliest centuries is one of the most amazing phenomena in all human history.

> The Gospel's impact was so profound that Christianity became the Roman Empire's official religion within just a few generations. When Constantine became a Christian, the Christian faith became the foundation of Western civilization[8]

Hearts prepared for the Gospel

The First Century hearers and recipients of the Gospel recognized and understood that Jesus alone could save man from his fallen condition because He alone can heal and restore the broken-hearted. Unfortunately, humanity is not unlike Humpty Dumpty in the old children's nursery rhyme, in that 'all the king's horses and all the king's men, couldn't put Humpty together again.' So, when a man's heart breaks, nothing can heal him apart from Jesus Christ. It is common in counseling situations, for example, to hear people tell of teenage heartbreak and the wounds people carry many decades later. In Mark's Gospel, it is no accident that the first person to whom Jesus showed himself alive after His resurrection was Mary Magdalene. This woman was one of Jesus' greatest supporters after He had cast out seven demons from her (Mark 16:9). No one could understand her appreciation for Jesus' help and saving work unless they had experienced the pain inflicted by demonic bondage or the sheer joy of complete deliverance from their past hurts and failures.

> The Spirit of the Lord GOD is upon Me because the LORD has anointed Me to preach good tidings to the poor; He has sent Me to heal the broken-hearted, to proclaim liberty to the captives, And the opening of the prison to those who are bound; Isaiah 61:1

In this prophecy regarding the messiah's work, the word broken-hearted describes those who have been crushed, hurt, shattered, and broken into pieces. It also has a secondary meaning of maimed, crippled, and wrecked—a reflection of much of the human condition down through the ages. In His hometown of Nazareth, doctor Luke recorded that Jesus had come to fulfill this prophecy. He had come to do for the human race what it could never do for itself. This is just as true today as it was in the First Century, where despite the vast technological progress and unprecedented affluence, Western Man is fundamentally unhappy. The human condition and its fundamental unhappiness have been expressed countless times in modern music. I think of the classic words of the Jimmy Ruffin song: "What becomes of the broken-hearted, who had love that's now departed?"

I will discuss in the next chapter the lack of inner peace in contemporary society and how it has led to an inability to be at peace with our fellow man. In the secularist society of man's creation, the best people can do is avoid pain and life's realities through endless escapism. Today, people seek to live out their lives vicariously in the life of their favorite screen heroes. Others seek to mask their pain with their drug of choice. For this reason, the legalization of harmful drugs has become popular amongst the political elites because, despite their claims of omnipotence, that is the best they can offer to the hurting masses.

The tragic suppression of the Gospel's truth (Romans 1:18) has led to a perception by those outside the Church that Christianity is dull and boring, but nothing could be further than the truth. Regardless of what the Church has become today, First Century society recognized those early believers living as an embodiment of the Gospel. The message proclamation of the resurrection of Jesus was the best news they would ever hear because it answers the deep cry of the human heart.

This encounter with the risen Savior had such a profound impact on man's heart that it ignited a movement against the darkness of the ancient world. And therefore, when rediscovered and taken seriously, it will ignite a similar transformation in the hearts of men and women today. Here are just a few of the truths that burst into flame to create the Gospel revolution of love:

Man coming home to God

The early church's message was that God created the universe, gave life to all things, and visited planet earth to show us the way home. Unfortunately, man's rebellion against God had caused separation, alienation, emptiness, and spiritual blindness, making the way home impossible. Despite man's protestations, he had rebelled against God, causing untold heartache by his callous disobedience. The only way forward was for God to send His son into the world to bring His lost sheep home. And so, the coming of Jesus marked the end of man's search for truth and meaning.

> God was in Christ reconciling the world to Himself, not imputing their trespasses to them, and has committed to us the word of reconciliation. 2 Corinthians 5:19

Man could never save himself, and for this reason, the angels announced the arrival of the fulfillment of man's greatest need—that is the birth of a savior. Thus, even though God was the aggrieved party, it was *He* who took the initiative through sacrificial love; to end the impasse and reconcile the human race to Himself.

> *Hark the herald angels sing*
> *"Glory to the newborn King!*
> *Peace on earth and mercy mild*
> *God and sinners reconciled"*
> *Joyful, all ye nations rise*
> *Join the triumph of the skies*
> *With the angelic host proclaim:*
> *"Christ is born in Bethlehem"*
> *Hark! The herald angels sing*
> *"Glory to the newborn King!"*
> —Charles Wesley (1707-1788)

The worth and value of the individual

Amongst the many, many things that the light of the Gospel was to reveal was the love of God and the worth and value of an individual. The Gospel revealed that we were created for a reason, and there is purpose in our existence. Having been created in the image of God, we are immensely precious in God's sight. God places so much value on the individual that Jesus was prepared to sacrifice His life to restore us to a relationship with Himself. This is at the heart of His plan of salvation. Ugandan Bishop Festo Kivengere (1919-1988) highlighted this profound truth when he said, 'You are not loved because you are important; you are important because you are loved.'

The claims of secularists are tragically false. The West's departure from its foundations in the Christian faith has resulted in people experiencing just how uncaring our society has become. Those who believe that God made people in His image will accord them the respect they deserve. Unfortunately, those who believe that human life began in the primordial ooze do not exhibit that same respect and often treat others with contempt.

Jesus enables Man to attain his fullest potential

God created us so that we are incomplete as individuals and can only experience the fullness of our humanity by living in a relationship with God and with others. Despite the modern quest for individualism, the need to love and be loved is the cry of every heart; it is an integral part of our humanity. By showing us the way from selfishness to love, Jesus enables people to be fully alive and truly human. This can only happen when we are motivated to surrender our independence and autonomy in favor of divine love. Just as a bride and groom relinquish independence for a committed relationship, Jesus' followers surrender their autonomy in favor of a love relationship with Him. For this reason, from the beginning, there has been a universal identification with the Gospel message. It seems strangely familiar, and when people heard it and responded, it felt as though they had come home.

> Man was so engineered by God that the presence of the Creator within the creature is indispensable to His humanity. Major Ian Thomas[9]

The Gospel of Jesus demonstrated that love is the most significant power in the universe. It is the only thing that can overcome man's selfishness and self-sufficiency. Jesus' saving work is the only way to turn selfishness to love and motivate humanity to put the interest of others before their own.

Having been created in God's image, we each have a spiritual nature and will never completely attain our fullest potential through worldly pursuits. Some claim that there is a God-shaped vacuum in every heart, suggesting that living in fellowship with God is hard-wired into our humanity.

We may receive eternal life from God

Man, made in God's image, screams out in protest against death. It seems so cruel and foreign that something as precious as a human life would end in death. Since the beginning of time, man has been challenged and confronted by his mortality. The various religions bear testimony to man's search for eternal life down through the ages, but Jesus Christ is the only person in history who has claimed to have conquered death and shown us the way to eternal life.

> But has now been revealed by the appearing of our Savior Jesus Christ, who has abolished death and brought life and immortality to light through the Gospel, 2 Timothy 1:10

Having been made in God's image, we each have an immortal soul that will live forever. Those who choose to reject God's way of salvation are condemning themselves to face death alone, followed by an eternity of separation from God that the Bible calls hell. Conversely, those who follow Jesus and His plan of salvation receive forgiveness of their sins and reconciliation with God. Thus, their destiny is to live in a place called heaven in God's eternal presence.

However, God's plan of salvation is not merely to save people from an eternity without God and the punishment and separation of hell; it is this and so much more. The mission of Jesus and the primary purpose of His saving work was, and is still, to restore man to God's image through the miracle of new birth. The former separation is remedied by a close relationship that the apostle Paul described as *'in Christ'*. Instead of separation, Jesus' followers experienced the miracle of the New Birth and the reality of, 'Christ *in* you the hope of Glory'.

> To them God willed to make known what are the riches of the glory of this mystery among the Gentiles: which is Christ in you, the hope of glory. Colossians 1:27

The Gospel message embraced so willingly by the first century Roman world comes to us fresh and new today. To a world seduced by materialism, sensual pleasure, and the lust for power, the message thunders down through the ages—this life is NOT all there is, you have a home in heaven waiting for you, and Jesus Christ is the only way home. Yet, this message, announced to a world shrouded in darkness, is still joyous good news today.

Mild He lays His glory by
Born that man no more may die
Born to raise the sons of earth
Born to give them second birth
Hark! The herald angels sing
"Glory to the newborn King!"
—Charles Wesley (1707-1788)

Jesus enables people to overcome the flaws of their humanity

One of the seductive delusions of our age has been the claim of the secularist religion that man is fundamentally blameless. Proponents believe that political intervention can remove inequalities, resulting in a beautiful era of enlightenment. Sadly, those seeking a political utopia insist on viewing the world as they would like it, choosing to overlook the reality. All human history attests to what the ancients like Cicero already knew—that man is his own worst enemy. More recently, social commentators have asked whether the real virus that afflicts us is not Covid-19 but rather man's primary condition. During the pandemic, many people selfishly spread the virus by placing their selfish interests above the welfare of others. This selfish sinfulness has proven the fatal flaw in our humanity throughout history, right up to the present time. Consequently, humans have been unable to attain its highest aspirations for freedom, love, joy, and peace on earth.

> The depravity of man is at once the most empirically verifiable reality but at the same time the most intellectually resisted fact.
> Malcolm Muggeridge (|1903-1990)[10]

The good news of Jesus is that He has provided a way; that is the *only* way for man to rise above his fatal flaw. This inherent flaw makes it impossible for man to pull himself up by his proverbial bootstraps because it requires a power outside himself. Only divine love is strong enough to overcome man's selfish sinfulness. The whole of history bears testimony to the grim reality that man, apart from God, can't save himself. Only the Gospel of Jesus enables individuals to rise above their fallen nature through God's divine enabling and become all that God intended us to be. The transforming power of the Gospel has been evidenced throughout history, whether in the life of Saul of Tarsus, who openly persecuted the church, or John Newton, the notorious slave trader who later wrote the classic hymn, *Amazing Grace*.

This inherent flaw makes it impossible for man to pull himself up by his own proverbial bootstraps because it requires a power outside of himself. Only divine love is strong enough to overcome man's selfish sinfulness

---

The Gospel's power is transformative because God Himself comes alongside our flawed humanity to regenerate, transform and provide a divine enabling for good. It is not just that the believer's sins are forgiven, but also because Jesus Christ resides in the heart through the Holy Spirit inspiring and empowering us to a higher life and existence than is possible apart from God.

The clash of light and darkness

The very nature of light is that it can't coexist with darkness because they are mutually exclusive. Light will always prevail. So, despite fierce opposition from the powers of darkness, the light of the Gospel prevailed and spread like wildfire throughout the ancient world. This established the foundation for the Gospel to profoundly impact and pervade Western civilization.

> The people who sat in darkness have seen a great light. And for those who lived in the land where death casts its shadow, a light has shined. Matthew 4:16 NLT

When the light of heaven came into our world to ignite the protest and pushback against the pagan darkness, it was inevitable that the empire of chaos would fight back. History is littered with examples of vested interests seeking to maintain their hold over the rights and freedoms of others. The response of paganism to the proclamation of the Gospel was as fierce as it was predictable. Alongside Biblical accounts of the birth of Jesus and the revelation of His love, the pushback from evil powers also appear. Reports of Jesus' birth concerned King Herod to such an extent that he ordered the slaughter of all male children under two, attempting to eliminate the threat to his power.[11]

So too the spread of the Gospel resulted in fierce opposition and intense persecution. This same struggle of light against darkness has been going on since the beginning of history and continues today. The outcome is inevitable as light always triumphs over darkness because darkness can never extinguish the light. It is this simple logic that makes a new pendulum swing of history, back to God, inevitable.

As Christianity spread and grew in popularity, so too did the persecution by the various Roman emperors. These harsh persecutions began with Nero and ended with the most brutal persecutions under Diocletian. To placate the public outcry because of the fire that had engulfed Rome, the emperor Nero (37-68 A.D.) used Christians as scapegoats and blamed them for this disaster. As a result, Christians were arrested and then killed in the Roman arenas, providing entertainment for the masses.

Some generations later, Diocletian (245-316 AD) sought to strengthen his crumbling regime by intense persecution of Jesus' followers. By the middle of the Third Century, the number of Christians had grown to an estimated 5 million.[12] The emperor believed that the only way to save his pagan empire was to eradicate Christianity. And so, Diocletian initiated no-holds-barred, all-out persecution to achieve his obscene goal. He destroyed Christian books and church buildings and arrested, tortured, and murdered those who refused to bow their knee to this self-proclaimed Roman demigod. Believers could choose to renounce their faith or die a violent and cruel death. The persecution was so brutal and violent that many pagans were shocked and appalled by the ferocity of the attacks.

Racks, scourges, swords, daggers, crosses, poison, and famine, were made use of in various parts to dispatch the Christians; and invention was exhausted to devise tortures against such as had no crime, but thinking differently from the votaries of superstition[13].

However, most Christians refused to accept Diocletian as a god and would not bow their knees to his authority. Their refusal developed into an all-out confrontation between light and darkness. The power of Rome was pitted against the love and grace of the followers of the Prince of peace. History records that the light prevailed, and Diocletian couldn't exterminate the Church. He was replaced by emperor Constantine (c.280-337 AD), who converted to Christianity. Finally, the might of Rome was compelled to bow its knee to the humble Galilean, and the world came to see that Jesus Christ truly is the king of kings and Lord of lords.

> History records that the light prevailed, and Diocletian couldn't exterminate the Church. He was replaced by emperor Constantine (c.280-337 AD), who converted to Christianity.

The foundation of western civilization

Irrespective of belief about God, it is a historical fact that Christianity provided Western civilization's spiritual and cultural foundations for almost 2,000 years. We will see in later chapters that it has been the departure from these foundations that have resulted in the inevitable decline of the West. Our post-modern, post-truth world is confused about everything, let alone something as complicated as what constitutes *civilization*. A traditional definition, written some time ago by C. Manning Clarke, is instructive. While not a believer, he understood the Christian worldview. He said civilization is 'the efforts made to ennoble, refine and cultivate the human personality by sublimating its instinctive nature'.[14] It is here that the Christian faith has made its superlative contribution to the establishment and advance of Western culture and civilization.

Both Christians and others acknowledge that the teachings of Jesus have profoundly influenced Western civilization. For example, before the introduction of the Gospel to what is now the United Kingdom, the region was inhabited by savage, barbaric people, even by Roman standards. While the Romans brought infrastructure such as roads and aqueducts to Britain, the later introduction of Christianity provided the civilizing influence of the Gospel to Western Europe.

> In the 1st Century AD, Britain had its own set of religious icons: Pagan gods of the earth and Roman gods of the sky. Into this superstitious and violent world came a modern, fashionable cult from the east: Christianity.[15] BBC

The Gospel's influence enabled the various tribes and regional kingdoms to unify through the Church and their shared faith in God. The Gospel roadmap delivered pagans from barbarism, allowing the West to thrive and progress. The Judeo-Christian worldview provided the cultural, legal, and social foundations of the West. The flag of the United Kingdom, for example, is an emblem of this unity. Displaying the crosses of their various patron saints, Saint Patrick, Saint Andrew, and Saint George, demonstrates the unifying effects of the Gospel. This flag is symbolic of the shared common ground between people from different languages and ethnic groups united in a common purpose. Sadly, the rejection of its Christian foundations with its unifying effect has resulted in the re-emergence of pre-Christian tribalism with its inevitable conflict and divisions.

Jesus used parables in His Sermon on the Mount to illustrate crucial universal truths. In one parable, He compares a wise man who built his house on the rock to a foolish one on a sand foundation. When the storms of life inevitably came, the house built on the rock stood firm. Whether it is an individual life or an entire civilization, the foundation's strength will determine success or failure. The rock-solid foundation of the West has been its respecting God's Word and compliance with His laws. Tragically, the West has rejected God as their foundation, relying instead on flawed human wisdom. Competing voices, each with a different interpretation of 'truth', inevitably lead to conflict. Once we enjoyed relative stability and calm, we can now expect escalating confusion.

> Therefore, whoever hears these sayings of Mine, and does them, I will liken him to a wise man who built his house on the rock: (Matthew 7:24)

Two

HEAVEN'S PEACE PLAN

> Because of God's tender mercy, the light from heaven is about to break upon us, to give light to those who sit in darkness and in the shadow of death, and to guide us to the path of peace. Luke 1:78-79 (NLT)

One factor contributing to the rejection of Western Christianity over the past 50 years has been the belief that man could establish world peace apart from God. The Peace Movement gained momentum in the baby-boomer generation after World War II from a sincere desire to avoid the conflicts of previous generations. Many from that generation viewed the Church as part of an established system that encouraged war and felt justified in turning their backs on God. However, instead of instituting a new age of enlightenment and world peace, Western society is torn by divisions, conflict, and increasing lawlessness with no human solution in sight. Its confusion about nearly everything has rendered it weak and unable to respond to the changed geopolitical situation and its threat to world peace.

I will outline what I am calling the Secularist Religion and the spiritual and social decline this has caused in the following chapter. For now, I will offer a simple illustration from a local newspaper that is typical of what we glean from the media every day. Reflecting on the social and cultural malaise and accompanying perplexity, a frequently asked question is, 'why are things the way they are?' I refer to an altercation between a cyclist and a pedestrian on a busy Melbourne street that stopped traffic, was caught on film, and made it onto a local TV news program. The presenter and a well-known social commentator covering the story referenced that this incident was symptomatic of a broader societal problem that is increasingly affecting us all. This news coverage left their viewers with two unanswered questions: why are people so angry, and what, if anything, can be done to remedy this growing problem? Their probing went unanswered as they were at a loss to provide an answer to either of these or other vital questions.

PRESENTER: "Gangs, public brawls, just so much anger, so much violence and vitriol, where's it coming from do you think?"

COMMENTATOR: "You've picked the right word there I think, why is everybody so angry? I don't know…"

PRESENTER: "I don't know but the violence, it's getting to the point where, you know, you're thinking twice about just walking down the street, you don't know what you are going to be confronted with".

COMMENTATOR: "It's going to continue until somehow we nail it down and **we are not getting anywhere**, not yet."[16] (Emphasis added)

I am using this violent incident on a Melbourne street to illustrate a recognized problem that remains unremedied—and there is a sense of perplexity and even powerlessness to address the root cause. There is no solution on offer, seemingly from either side of politics or the political commentators with their vast army of social pundits.

The lack of solutions to societal problems is compounded in many cases by the failure of politicians to even listen to people's concerns. Our political system led us to believe that democracy was about having a voice representing the people's interests. There is, however, an increasing view that both the left and the right-wing of the political classes appear to be willfully ignorant of their people's concerns. Instead, they seem more committed to their careers and self-interest, kowtowing to powerful vested interests. Whatever the reasons, politicians are increasingly seen as a part of the problem. As a result, voters move further to the left or the right out of sheer frustration.

This present reality reminds us that humanity's only hope lies in the salvation offered by Jesus Christ. Accordingly, there needs to be a recognition and declaration both outside and inside the Church of heaven's peace plan.

The angelic announcement of peace on Earth

When the angels heralded Jesus' birth to the shepherds on that first Christmas Day, it was supremely an announcement of God's good intentions for planet earth. The Creator of heaven and earth came with a message of peace to a world that had lost its way. The angels rejoiced when Jesus was born in Bethlehem because the long-awaited Messiah of the Jewish people had arrived.

God stepped down into history in what the Bible calls 'the fullness of time' (Galatians 4:4). The time was right. Jesus was not only the promised Jewish Messiah but also the Savior of the whole world. Jesus came on a divine mission that was, humanly speaking—mission impossible. He was sent from heaven to planet earth to bring people home to God that didn't want to go home. Jesus came to rescue a world that didn't, for the most part, want to be rescued. Due to their innate selfishness, they didn't want Him at all. Jesus coming was about heaven reaching down in love to people who were in rebellion against God and heavily invested in their independence and autonomy.

> Jesus came to rescue a world that didn't—for the most part, want to be rescued and who, because of their innate selfishness, didn't really want him at all.

The Gospel message is that beyond this physical world that we interface through our senses, there is also an invisible spiritual world that is even more real. Not only that, but as the story unfolded, it became apparent that the existing world system was ruled by spiritually blind people who didn't want to know about the kingdom of heaven that was about to be established in the hearts of men. King Herod was willing to slaughter innocent babies in a futile attempt to preserve his despotic kingdom. These petty, self-serving kingdoms have blighted humanity and generated much hatred and violence down through the ages. Legitimate, meaningful peace on earth can only come through the reign of the Prince of Peace in the hearts of men.

The angels rejoiced when Jesus was born in Bethlehem because the long-awaited Jewish Messiah and the Savior of the entire world had now arrived.

It is doubtful whether even the angels understood the full extent of what they saw unfold before them. Even today, the whole meaning of Jesus' coming is not fully appreciated even by those who follow Him. It has taken 2,000 years of unfolding world history to teach the human race that this world needs a savior because man is incapable of saving himself. The birth of Jesus was God's gift of peace to planet earth and the situation in our world today makes this message even more relevant and urgent than ever before.

> And suddenly there was with the angel a multitude of the heavenly host praising God and saying: "Glory to God in the highest, And on earth peace, goodwill toward men!" Luke 2:13-14

The Christmas truce

Whenever I think of the Christmas story and the angelic announcement from heaven of 'peace on earth', I usually think of the Christmas Truce from

World War 1. On Christmas Eve 1914, both German and Allied soldiers put their war aside to celebrate Christmas together. They laid down their weapons, left the safety of their trenches, shook hands, exchanged gifts, sang Christmas Carols, and even played soccer together. However, it was not long before this spontaneous expression of goodwill ended, and their military masters ordered them back into the trenches to continue to fight their debauched, inhuman war. One firsthand account indicates that the Germans started the peace initiative in their sector when they erected Christmas trees complete with candles and signs displaying in broken English 'YOU NO FIGHT, WE NO FIGHT'. This remarkable display of humanity amid a brutal and bloody conflict demonstrated the power of love to transform and bring peace on earth: even if only for a fleeting moment.

> Then, they exchanged gifts. Chocolate cake, cognac, postcards, newspapers, tobacco. In a few places, along the trenches, soldiers exchanged rifles for soccer balls and began to play games.[18]

In this poignant, true story, it was the soldier's belief in God and the sacredness of the Christmas tradition that eclipsed the hatred, conflict and violence of war. God's love prevailed over their base human nature. It was their faith and belief in Jesus that empowered them, even if only for a few hours, to lay aside the insane hostility caused by their leader's lust for power and their nonsensical geopolitical agendas. For just a moment, their humanity and faith transcended the inhuman madness of war. The kingdom of God superseded the kingdom of man.

The need for peace today

Despite man's best efforts, our world today is still one of conflict and division, with an increasingly hostile environment. Experts from various fields inform us that peace on earth is just as elusive as ever. The present geopolitical landscape is increasingly like that in Europe before the outbreak of World War I. Neither the League of Nations nor the United Nations have prevented the rise of radical Islamic Terrorism or the hostility of Communist China and North Korea. Russia is also testing the patience of the free world in Europe with no sign of any positive changes in the foreseeable future. It appears that these anti-Western regimes view the West's reluctance to defend human freedoms as a sign of their confusion and weakness. The Global

Peace Index scientifically measures the levels of peace in our world, and its data reveals that from 2018 to 2020, the level of world peace dropped by 2.5%.

So too, the Bulletin of Atomic Scientists tell us that in 2020, the Doomsday Clock was a mere 100 seconds to midnight. As well as the danger from external threats, the West is trying to deal with internal conflict and division. Having rejected its Christian heritage and with it the glue that previously held society together—Western civilization is now so deeply divided that it cannot agree on dealing with internal malaise or external threats. Moreover, the West's secularization is so complete that even Christmas celebrations have little to do with the birth of Jesus and heaven's peace plan.

The West has been in tight spots before, but it had a roadmap and moral compass to assist navigation. Unfortunately, our current moral and social confusion has resulted in the West ignoring or appeasing its enemies. Still, history shows that this is never an acceptable solution to conflict. Giving aggressors what they want will always be a sign of weakness that strengthens their resolve to assert their will and impose their agenda on those weaker than themselves.

The peace that the angels announced at the birth of Christ goes beyond appeasement and the absence of conflict. Heaven's peace is a reality that God continues to communicate to earth over millennia. The Hebrew word Shalom is used in the Bible to depict the idea of peace and wellbeing. This profound word is still used as a form of greeting by Jewish people today. The concept of Shalom goes beyond the cessation of conflict; it incorporates welfare and wellbeing together with all our human necessities provided in abundance. It goes beyond mere economic interest to include the deep needs of the human heart as people live together in harmony. Shalom is that it is something not inherent in human nature—it is something that only God can give.

> The LORD will give strength to His people; The LORD will bless His people with peace. Psalms 29:11

The notion of peace on earth was foreign to the pagan Roman world, whose population worshipped the gods of war and venerated the concept of power and might. History records only strife, friction, and wars from one generation to another, despite man's yearning for something better. And it was for this reason that Jesus came as our peacemaker. Until Jesus came, no one challenged the might-makes-right rule of the Roman rulers because despotic Caesarism was the logical outcome of paganism. By contrast, the power of God's kingdom in the human heart is the source of all of heaven's blessings, with peace as the outcome.

Jesus came as the Savior of the world to do for us what we could never do for ourselves. Among the many prophecies concerning Jesus' advent, Isaiah predicted that the Messiah would be known as the Prince of Peace, indicating that, unlike earthly rulers, His reign would result in perfect peace and God-given Shalom.

> For unto us a Child is born, unto us a Son is given; and the government will be upon His shoulder. And His name will be called Wonderful, Counselor, Mighty God, Everlasting Father, Prince of Peace. Isaiah 9:6

In the previous chapter, we saw why the Gospel of Jesus profoundly impacted the first-century pagan Roman world. The Gospel of Jesus alone provides a way for man to live in peace with God, himself, and others. Peace on earth begins with peace with God. Only when man is at peace with God can he know deep and abiding inner peace and contentment and enjoy peace with his fellow man. Peace on earth is achievable, but only when individuals cooperate with their Maker. They must allow Him to impart His peace – a state that goes way beyond anything man can imagine, let alone find by himself. There is no other way. And so, it is that Heaven's Peace Plan teaches us that:

- Jesus is the only way to peace with God
- Jesus is the only way to inner peace in the human heart
- Jesus is the only way to peace on earth.

Jesus is the way to peace with God.

The history of the world records the tragic consequences of man's rebellion against God and His laws; constant war, upheaval, pain, and suffering. Hence, peace on earth must begin with peace with God. Throughout his long ministry as an evangelist, Dr Billy Graham (1918-2018) emphasized that humanity's problem is spiritual because our revolt severed our relationship with God.[19] Before we can experience peace in our hearts, we must first make peace with God. Jesus' mission was to provide a pathway to peace with God.

Jesus crucifixion testifies to God's love for a lost and confused world. His death on a Cross is black and white. There can be no debate or conjecture. We must choose to accept or reject God's love. Just as Jesus' golden rule ('just as you want men to do to you, you also do to them likewise'. Luke 6:31) is the highest moral standard in the universe, so too is His self-sacrifice the highest expression of love imaginable. Jesus taught his disciples that there is no greater love than for a man to lay down his life for his friends (John 15:13). The apostle Paul and others later discovered that Jesus didn't only die for His friends but also for those who hated Him and wanted him dead. Jesus didn't just talk about love—He demonstrated His divine love by His death on the Cross. His sacrificial love contrasted with the values of the pagan world of the first century A.D. and ignited a protest against the darkness of paganism that continues today.

The first issue Jesus addressed was man's separation from God. God gave His law to Moses as a roadmap for life. By keeping God's Law and walking in His ways, man could enjoy the Shalom God had promised His people for many generations. The problem was, and still is, that man's propensity for selfishness prevented him from keeping God's Law and living the way He intended. So, Jesus came as the Savior of His people, first to offer His life as a sacrifice to pay our debt to God, and secondly to turn people from selfishness to love.

The first step in God's peace process was to deal with His holy law, which required payment of the penalty for man's sin. From the opening chapters of the Bible, God initiated a system of sacrifices to atone for sin. When Isaiah prophesied the coming of the Messiah, he claimed that He would be 'despised and rejected' by the people.[20] The great irony was that despite the Messiah being vilified, rejected, and persecuted, His suffering and sacrificial love would pave the way for their salvation. In one of the most profound eternal truths, we see that as an act of selfless love, the Messiah would take on his shoulders the sins of the world.[21] In what theologians have called the substitutionary atonement, Jesus' death paid the price for my sins and yours. The Gospel message is that no matter how much we may have rebelled against God and broken His heart by our disobedience, He is willing to forgive us because of Jesus' sacrificial act. Because of what Jesus has done for us, we can experience peace with God.

> Therefore, having been justified by faith, we have peace with God through our Lord Jesus Christ, Romans 5:1

Jesus came to earth as a man to fulfill all the requirements of God's Law and open the door between heaven and earth. This was something only hinted at in the Old Testament Tabernacle where mortal man could call on a Holy God in prayer. He alone could broker a peace deal between heaven and earth and make the way open for us to return home to God.

Down through the centuries, countless millions of people have willingly and joyously chosen to follow Jesus. While not everyone understands the profound theological implications of God's actions, even a child can know that He loves us and can forgive our sins.

The message of the Cross is central to and the very essence of the Gospel. As an act of supreme love and sacrifice, Jesus died for the sins of the world. By perfectly obeying God's righteous law and fulfilling its demand for justice, Jesus paid the price for sin and made peace with God possible. This is a truth so simple anyone can comprehend it but so profound that it has challenged the greatest intellects of the ages. As Charles Wesley (1707-1788) wrote during the First Great Awakening, "Tis mystery all! The immortal dies! Who can explore His strange design? In vain the firstborn seraph tries to sound the depths of love Divine!"[22]

When we view history from the Judeo-Christian perspective, we see that man's rebellion against God and his desire to replace Him with idols of his own making has been the source of all the world's pain and misery. Conversely, man's peace and well-being have flowed from making peace with God and walking in His ways. Right living produces peace and harmony, while rebellion against God's law produces pain, misery, and death. In God's peace plan, righteousness and peace go together.

> Mercy and truth have met together; Righteousness and peace have kissed. Psalms 85:10

It is only in relationship with our Maker that we will experience the full measure of our humanity and discover the purpose for which we were created. Jesus alone can fulfill the deep desires of the human heart and our aspirations for 'something more'. As well as showing us the way home to God, it is divine love alone that can transform the human heart from selfishness to love. It is this heavenly love that changes God's enemies into His friends. Additionally, as well as being His friends, He adopts His followers into His family as his dear children.

When man rebelled against God's laws, it broke His heart. Not only our actions have offended God, but also our hurtful and belligerent attitude caused affront. Hurts from broken relationships do not heal easily, and it was costly for the Father to send Jesus to die on the Cross. The problem was there was no one else who could do the job, and as the words of an old children's hymn remind us:

> There was no other good enough, to pay the price of sin;
> He only could unlock the gate of heaven and let us in. Cecil Alexander (1818-1895) [23]

A child's rebellion against their parent's love is a heinous thing, and so is our rebellion against our heavenly Father. But as severe as our sin against our Father's love is, Jesus' blood has paid the price and opened the door to peace with God. We could never do enough to make restitution to God, but the amazing grace of the Gospel is that Jesus died to secure our forgiveness.

And it is because of Jesus' sacrifice we can experience peace with God. We may not understand it entirely, but we can still accept it by faith in God's Word. This is where Heaven's Peace Plan begins.

Jesus is the Way to peace in the human heart

Once we have made peace with God and have stopped resisting Him, the way is open to experience real peace in our hearts. Soon after becoming a follower of Jesus, I vividly remember sitting in an armchair with a deep, wonderful peace in my heart. My foot was no longer tapping nervously, and the demons that drove me were gone. I had never known such peace before, and even today, it is impossible to describe it adequately. The apostle Paul said that the peace that God bestows is beyond all human understanding.[24] In personal experience, the pain and hurt were gone, so too was the manic non-stop drive of trying to prove myself and justify my actions. I was no longer what someone described as 'a walking civil war'. The war was over—I had made peace with God. I was, at last, enjoying a deep abiding peace in my heart, indescribable to anyone who has never experienced it themselves.

> Every man is a walking civil war. Within him there is the tension, the division, the battle between right and wrong, between good and evil, between passion and reason, between the instincts and the will. William Barclay [25]

This search for inner peace and meaning has continued since the dawn of recorded history, but the answer is still the same despite recent technological progress. The state of the world today only makes it even more apparent that the fundamental problem with humanity is man himself and that he is still his own worst enemy.

People do things, sometimes in ignorance and sometimes intentionally that are just plain stupid! Nowhere is this seen more clearly than the West's rejection of Jesus Christ and with this, all the blessing of peace with God that He offers.

Having rejected the Gospel and God's rightful place in their lives, people have pursued lifestyles that pander to their fallen humanity. In doing so, they have embraced a pagan worldview. Doomed to making moral decisions using their corrupt nature, they have become like Atlas, a mythological demigod who defied his superiors who condemned him to carry the world on his shoulders. This story from pagan mythology paints a vivid picture of how when people rebel against God, they become solely responsible for their welfare, a heavy burden of responsibility it was never intended we carry. It is no wonder that people in the West are so stressed, anxious, and fearful, seeking to mask their pain with drugs, while suicide is at epidemic levels.

> There is inner tension. Men live a distracted life, for the word distract literally means to pull apart. So long as a man is a walking civil war and a split personality, there can obviously be for him no such thing as serenity. There is only one way out of this, and that is for self to abdicate to Christ. When Christ controls, the tension is gone. William Barclay [26]

Being free from God's rules and laws may seem like a good idea, but it is too easy to make bad decisions, get it wrong and mess things up. Without God's roadmap for life, we must figure it out independently. That is problematic because even if we had ten lifetimes, that wouldn't be long enough to figure everything out. But none of us has ten lifetimes! We only have one, and life can become painful and dysfunctional when we mess it up. For this reason, God sent his only Son, Jesus Christ, to come to planet earth as the Savior of the world.

> For God so loved the world that He gave His only begotten Son, that whoever believes in Him should not perish but have everlasting life. John 3:16

When we make peace with God, everything begins to improve as the Prince of Peace works in our hearts. Then, we can get on with living and let God get on with His business of running the universe! Once we stop defying God, we can stop condemning ourselves and beating ourselves up over things that we have no power to change. The apostle Paul teaches that when Jesus rules our lives, God's peace will also reign in our hearts. Then we can personally experience 'the peace of God that passes all understanding' (Philippians 4:7).

Jesus is the way to peace with others.

Heaven's Peace Plan is increasingly relevant in an age when Western society is deeply divided and conflicted. There is no other way. When we make our peace with God and allow Him to rule our lives, He will fill us with His love and enrich our other relationships. By contrast, if we choose to keep fighting with God, we will never be at peace with ourselves, and the rest of the world will suffer! Isn't it true that we tend to take it out on others when we are angry or upset with ourselves? We offer all manner of polite explanations for our bad temper and say we are out of sorts or having a bad hair day or something like that, but the truth is that this is just our inner turmoil manifesting itself.

> Heaven's Peace Plan begins with saving us from our selfish sinfulness, and this frees us from building our petty little kingdoms. Only then can we relate to our fellow human beings as brothers and sisters instead of rivals in an age-old cosmic power struggle. This is only possible by the manifestation and sacrifice of divine love.

When Jesus taught the Golden Rule, He explained that this was not some new teaching but a reminder of what we already know instinctively. When God gave his law to Moses on Mount Sinai, He set in stone the moral laws previously written on the heart of man and implanted in our DNA.

> Therefore, whatever you want men to do to you, do also to them, for this is the Law and the Prophets. Matthew 7:12

Understanding these laws and agreeing with them is one thing but living them is another thing entirely—therefore, we need Jesus as our enabling Savior. To love others in the same way we love ourselves, we must first experience inner peace, which can only happen when we are at peace with God. The law stipulated what we ought to do, but it is only through the power of the Gospel that our hearts convert from selfishness to love. Paganism is the outworking of man's selfish sinfulness, whereas God transforms our hearts as He fulfills His promise to write His law in the hearts of his people.[28]

The law stipulated what we *ought* to do,
but it is only through the power of the Gospel
that our hearts convert from selfishness to love.

We were all created to live in a relationship with others, so it makes no sense to reject what the apostle James called God's Royal Law that stipulates, 'You shall love your neighbor as yourself,' (James 2:8). God designed the Law that He gave His people as a roadmap to life so we could experience His favor and live in peace. The Apostle Paul explained that 'all the law is fulfilled in one word, even in this: 'You shall love your neighbor as yourself' (Galatians 5:14). Just as the natural laws govern our universe, God gave the moral Law so people could live together in peace and harmony. Just as our planet orbits in perfect synchronization around the Sun, so too can our human existence only ever reach its full measure in a love relationship with our Maker. Love is the fulfillment of the Law, and it is the glue that holds everything together. Sir Isaac Newton and others observed a simple logic that if the Lord had established the universe and fixed the stars by his 'wise counsel',[29] then it makes perfect sense to follow the laws that our Maker has given to his people. If ever planet earth decided to pursue a more independent trajectory and somehow break free of its orbit around the Sun, all life on planet earth would expire. Our planet would veer off into the cosmic darkness of outer space, and all life on earth would cease.

# PART TWO

THE SPIRITUAL TIDE IN THE WEST IS OUT

Three

THE NEED FOR REVIVAL TODAY

> To destroy a people, you must first sever their roots.
> Aleksandr Solzhenitsyn (1918-2008)

The bait and switch con job

The bait and switch con is when a punter is offered a quality item for sale at a significantly reduced price. However, when he takes delivery, he finds a fake—not what he paid for—the anticipated bargain turns out to be an expensive counterfeit. Anyone who has traveled will have noticed the 'bargains' offered and the incredibly low prices for sportswear and other goods. Experienced travelers know that although these so-called 'bargain' items may look the same and even exhibit brand-name credentials, they are rarely genuine items. The con works due to our human nature; we all like a bargain and desperately want to believe the fakes are genuine articles.

> The willingness to buy into the delusion overrides our exercise of caution and common sense. Our adult experience teaches us that if something appears too good to be true; it generally is

But people get conned because they want it to be true. They take the risk—and suffer accordingly.

At its heart, the appeal of secularism is that it promised all the benefits of the Christian faith but without the God stuff, and the moral price tag. They wanted all the blessings of liberal democracy but at a bargain-basement price. Each of the various strands of secularism offered the dream of a wonderful utopian golden age without the constraints of the traditional rules, boundaries, and conditions. Unfortunately, the West now must come to grips with the ramifications of buying into the secularist delusion—and getting conned. The West has willingly surrendered almost 2,000 years of Christian heritage in exchange for a man-made counterfeit. It has exchanged the worship of God for trust in man's abilities to order society and address those things that challenge our welfare. Tragically, however, this new religion hasn't ushered in a new age of peace and harmony but has returned to the old pre-Christian paganism.

While I refer to secularism as a religion, I must be fair and point out that secularists themselves have asserted their rejection of religion and the belief in the supernatural. English secularists, for example, have stated clearly: 'secularism seeks to interpret life on principles taken solely from the material world, without recourse to religion.' Despite these protestations, I have no hesitation in using the word Religion to describe secularism, as it is absolutely a faith-based system. It is, however, still a religion, albeit one based on their worship of man. They have replaced the worship of God with the deification of man despite his obvious flaws and shortcomings. Their belief in man's abilities to solve society's problems is predicated on their faith in the omniscience and omnipotence of man.

Putting their faith in man's abilities to solve his problems, considering all history, is a huge step of faith! This is not a matter of semantics. Secularists themselves have expressed their confidence in their movement in religious terms. The flavor of the Humanist Manifesto I was religious in tone. One of the signatories, William Floyd referred to it as 'the religious philosophy of humanism.

> The religious philosophy of humanism as a substitute for metaphysical theology will enable men to realize the highest value in life without surrendering their minds to any final dogma or any alleged revelation of the supernatural. [31] William Floyd

What I would call the Secularist Religion is not about one set of ideologies but rather a stitched-together Frankenstein monster of ideas from several different sources. Secular humanism, cultural Marxism, and New Age Religion are the main strands of this religion, and each of these has religious or quasi-religious roots. In each case, their beginnings go back to the heady days of the Victorian era, at the height of the West's spiritual, social, and technological progress. The advancements of the Victorian age created egotistical pride and hubris that made people think that man was both omnipotent and omniscient. They sincerely believed that there was nothing man couldn't do if he put his mind to it. This mindset and worldview promoted the idea of establishing a society independently from God.

> Glory to Man in the highest! For Man is the master of things.
> Algernon Charles Swinburne (1837-1909)

Sadly, the Victorian notions of man overcoming all his problems proved delusory, as the outbreak of World War I showed. This was not the war that would end all wars. Just before the outbreak of the Great War the sinking of the Titanic in 1912 had already begun to expose the delusion of man's claims to omnipotence. The ship was so technologically advanced it was pronounced unsinkable—until that is, it hit the hard, cold reality of an iceberg. So too, the new age of enlightenment and love that Secularism promised is now exposed for the delusion it is. The decline of the West has dispelled all notions of man's claims of deity. Under the guise of progress and being progressive, the West has chosen to reject God's authority and replaced it with a confederacy of ideas with its man-made rules and regulations. This is idolatry pure and simple with the substitution of the worship of man-made idols in place of God.

> The kings of the earth set themselves, And the rulers take counsel together, against the LORD and against His Anointed, saying, "Let us break Their bonds in pieces and cast away Their cords from us." Psalm 2:2-3

Only when we understand the spiritual nature of undermining the Christian worldview will we see the extent of the problem. As the apostle Paul said, 'we are not fighting against people made of flesh and blood' (Ephesians 6:12 NLT). This means that the secularists who oppose us are not our real enemy. They are, as Jesus said, merely 'the blind leading the blind' (Matthew 15:14). Behind the bid to remove the Christian foundations of Western society are invisible spiritual powers of darkness that the apostle Paul described as, 'the rulers of the darkness of this age, against spiritual hosts of wickedness in the heavenly places (Ephesians 6:12).

For the most part, the Church has been unable to turn the tide of the encroaching darkness for several generations because it has failed to recognize the spiritual nature of its conflict. When, however, the Church wakes up to the spiritual battle it is engaged in, it will also be able to realize that it has immense spiritual resources available to which the powers of darkness have no answer. Just as in the first century, the contemporary Church also has defensive armor and resources to survive and prevail in this universal struggle of light against the present darkness. Only when we understand the epic dimensions of our struggle and our human impotence to stand against the onslaught will we humble ourselves and seek the Lord for his help. This is where the turning of the tide of godlessness begins.

History records countless examples of man's ingenuity in devising schemes to escape from God, including God-substitutes and alternative religions. Their common goal was to avoid God's authority. An early attempt recorded in scripture was the construction of the Tower of Babel, driven by the same motivations that surround us today.

Some symptoms of the West's malaise

Malaise is a general illness whose exact cause is unknown or difficult to diagnose. This sums up the condition of those living in the West at this time when, despite unprecedented levels of freedom and affluence, people appear increasingly unhappy. This unhappiness is just one symptom of a general feeling of being unwell, symptomatic of a severe underlying problem. Anyone who lived through the COVID-19 pandemic or the 2020 US Presidential elections would doubt this condition exists.

The urgency of the present situation is compounded by the fact that while the West has faced existential crises before, there was the traditional moral compass to guide the way. Unfortunately, this is no longer the case.

The malaise requires an accurate diagnosis before effective treatment is possible. Cancer patients need the best treatment medical science can provide, not some New Age hocus-pocus. Blame for the current malaise has been attributed to city living, but these same problems are evident in rural and semi-rural communities. Karl Marx, primarily an economist, believed that the rest would take care of itself when people were better off economically. Despite unprecedented levels of affluence, however, people in the West today are, in general, very unhappy.

> I think everybody should get rich and famous and do everything they ever dreamed of so they can see that it's not the answer.
> Jim Carrey [32]

The idea of autonomy from God has a certain appeal, but it condemns people to navigate through life with only their limited personal experience for guidance. Having rejected God and His roadmap for life, people are left to figure out the meaning of life by themselves. Some are more successful at this than others. Each stage of life has unique challenges for which we are unprepared due to inexperience. It can take a long time to figure 'life' out—some people never do.

Having rejected the Gospel and God's rightful place in their lives, people have pursued lifestyles that pander to their fallen humanity. In doing so, they have embraced a pagan worldview. Doomed to making moral decisions using their corrupt nature, they have become like Atlas, a mythological demigod who defied his superiors who condemned him to carry the world on his shoulders. This story from pagan mythology paints a vivid picture of how when people rebel against God, they become solely responsible for their welfare, a heavy burden of responsibility never intended. It is no wonder that people in the West are so stressed, anxious and fearful, seeking to mask their pain with drugs, while suicide is at epidemic levels.

> There is inner tension. Men live a distracted life, for the word distract literally means to pull apart. So long as a man is a walking civil war and a split personality, there can obviously be for him no such thing as serenity. There is only one way out of this, and that is for self to abdicate to Christ. When Christ controls, the tension is gone. William Barclay [33]

In previous generations, people in the West
held on to the hope of life after death.
Today people seem confused about life before death

The Western obsession with materialism, sensual enjoyment and consumerism means that whole generations have condemned themselves to an existence that is the human equivalent of battery hens. Technological progress seeks to discover how to mask people's pain so they can self-medicate with their painkiller of choice.

The symptoms of Western malaise originate in man's heart and then overflow to the broader community. The internal symptoms of dis-ease and unhappiness in the individual spirit include the loneliness epidemic resulting from the alienation that health professionals are saying is just as deadly as smoking. So too the growing levels of addiction to pornography. Instead of the win-win plan for marriage that God's laws outlined, the worship of the pagan deities of sex has become a lose-lose proposition, with both men and women feeling cheated. Because of this, many women increasingly see 'all men as losers', and men are turning to pornography and sex workers for fulfillment at an alarming rate.

Yet another symptom of the Western malaise is the drug abuse epidemic involving both prescription and non-prescription drugs. Despite the harmful effects of drug abuse, there has been widespread confusion about handling this epidemic. Some treat the problem as a law enforcement issue, while others advocate the legalization of all drugs. No one seems to be asking serious questions about the origin of the pain people seek to mask through this activity. Alongside the drug problem, there is also a suicide epidemic. A 2013 Newsweek article reported that 400,000 people in America alone took their lives in just one decade. That is similar to the number of Americans who died in World War II and Korea combined. I can see no evidence that this problem has been addressed and remedied. The only trend that I can discern is that people today commit suicide at an even younger age.

The external symptoms of the internal disorder include erosion of civility, cyber-bullying, the rise of road and air rage, and an increase in violent crime. These problems result from the inner human turmoil experienced by people out of fellowship with God being inflicted on the broader society. No amount of social engineering or gender-neutral language can heal the deep hurts of the human heart. Only God can do that, which is why we need a Savior. Unfortunately, neither right-wing nor left-wing politicians have answers for the deep divisions in Western society. All the observable data point to things getting worse.

> Materialism, the most boring as well as the least accurate way of experiencing the world and recording experience, is the dominant mindset of the Western intelligentsia in our day.
> A.N. Wilson [34]

Having jettisoned its traditional roadmap, each individual, group, and tribe must figure out their own identity, a prescription for chaos. Having rejected Jesus' Golden Rule, everything becomes a power struggle, and the law of the jungle prevails. With no unifying factor, no glue to hold society together, people are increasingly tribal, supporting those who think alike and attacking those who disagree. Sensing that others who don't see things their way aren't listening and don't care, they gravitate towards like-minded people who think the same way. Conflict is inevitable when tribes see each other as enemies. This new tribal-based paganism threatens individual welfare and, with it, the destruction of Western civilization as we know it.

During the American Civil War, President Abraham Lincoln (1809-1865) quoted a timeless pearl of wisdom from Jesus, who said, "every city or house divided against itself will not stand." President Lincoln paraphrased this quotation when he said: 'a house divided against itself cannot stand'.[35]

> Every kingdom divided against itself is brought to desolation,
> and every city or house divided against itself will not stand.
> Matthew 12:25

Jesus' statement is universally true. If, for example, married people fight each other, both partners lose out, and the union will most likely fail. This is true of every social contract, whether a local family or broader society. If one part of a society is fighting against another, then that nation will be conflicted and wither. By abandoning truths that prospered our civilization, the West is committing cultural suicide—and with disastrous consequences.

> Everybody feels the evil, but no one has courage or energy
> enough to seek the cure. Alexis de Tocqueville, (1805-1859)
> Democracy in America

Despite the dominance of secularism, most of the population still believes there must be something more to life than mere animal existence. Although the Western church has failed to counter secularism in the past few generations, there remains a thirst for something more that our Creator has hardwired into our DNA. Once the West begins to wake up to its present predicament, we should expect to see a widespread protest and reset. If these facts alone don't drive the Church to its knees to call out to God for an Awakening today, I don't know what else will. There must be a revival in the Church before there can be an awakening in our society. Opinions may differ whether this will occur outside or inside the church, but the light of the Gospel continues to shine, and the darkness can never extinguish it.

> To look out at this kind of creation out here and not believe
> in God is to me impossible. John Glenn (1921-2016),
> Astronaut

The decline of the West

History teaches us that civilizations rise and fall, and by every indicator, Western civilization has seen its best days and is in severe decline. Despite its claims of progress, our culture is showing symptoms of severe malaise. From being the light on the hill and envy of nations, it is confused about everything, including its own identity and direction. Unlike previous generations, people in the West no longer imagine happy days and a bright tomorrow, and the future is often described in apocalyptic terms. Hope for the future through God's kingdom has been almost completely forgotten. By contrast, the realms of man leave little room for hope. Other nations can see it, and the West's enemies take advantage of this confusion, but so many of our population are so out of touch with reality that they don't want to see or face the obvious.

> Research shows the automatic assumption of a better future for citizens in the west has now gone. [36] Dr. Robert Skidelsky

The reasons for the decline of the West are both obvious and reversible. The Gospel of Jesus produced the greatest reset in history to become the foundation of Western civilization. I offer a traditional definition of civilization as 'the efforts made to ennoble, refine and cultivate the human personality by sublimating its instinctive nature.' Historically, the Gospel provided a pathway out of pagan barbarism, resulting in tribes and regional kingdoms united by their shared faith in God. If it was the Gospel of Jesus that gave life and structure to Western civilization, it stands to reason that removing these foundations has resulted in the decline of the West. The Gospel of Jesus gave the West its spiritual and cultural foundations. The current deterioration is simply the consequential outcome of removing these foundations.

> Without religion there can be no morality, and without morality there can be no law. Lord Denning (1899-1999) [37]

The warnings of Oswald Spengler

In 1918, historian and philosopher Oswald Spengler published The Decline of the West and trumpeted the warning that Western civilization manifested the symptoms of a fatal decline.

To illustrate his ideas, Spengler examined eight civilizations that had been the dominant superpowers of their day: each of these civilizations was born, grew strong, and then died. His study included the Egyptian, Greek, and Roman Empires that each went through phases or seasons—'spring', 'summer', 'autumn', and 'winter' phases that Spengler used to illustrate their rise and fall. Applying this same template to Western civilization, Spengler showed convincingly that the West had passed its spring and summer high points and was now on a downward phase. It had now entered the winter or death cycle.

> Spengler explained that the winter or death cycle of any civilization happens when it loses the principle or dynamic that gave it birth

Spengler was writing at the end of the Victorian summer as it gave way to autumn, which was soon to be followed by the winter or death phase of the West. The Victorian era's technological and social advancement promoted feelings of hubris and human invincibility—that man had within his grasp the ability to establish a utopia. These advancements generated an arrogance that believed God's Law could be set aside and the teachings of Jesus ignored. Any illusions man could establish a utopian society apart from God were soon shattered.

The carnage of World War I became the writing on the wall for the West as it conclusively showed man's need for God more than ever before. British Prime Minister David Lloyd-George (1863-1945) recognized that the deep-seated problems in our world are beyond the ability of man to address. Leading Britain at the end of the war, he admitted that the 'War to end all wars' had not solved any of the problems it was seeking to address. The Allied defeat of Germany only inflated the hubris and pride of the victors and sought to humiliate the vanquished that, in hindsight, made World War II inevitable. Only Heaven's peace plan can bring peace on earth, but the teachings of Jesus were set aside, and Germany was to embrace the pagan Wagnerian gods of war for yet another generation.

> David Lloyd George, Earl of Dwyfor, then Prime Minister of Britain, frankly confessed, after World War I, that "nothing less than a great spiritual awakening among the nations could possibly enable the leaders to iron out the appalling difficulties harassing their minds day and night." [38]

With almost prophetic insight, Oswald Spengler viewed the events of World War I and the subsequent aftermath as an indication that Western Civilization was in its winter or death phase. The West had forsaken those things that gave it life—and because of this, death was inevitable. Having rejected the Golden Rule of loving their neighbor as themselves, the seeds of pagan darkness would once more prevail, and the writing was on the wall for the future wellbeing of the West.

> Without an equal growth of Mercy, Pity, Peace, and Love, Science herself may destroy all that makes human life majestic and tolerable. Sir Winston Churchill (1874-1965) [39]

The death principle

When God gave His Law to Moses, it came with a warning. Following and obeying God's laws would result in His blessing and bring life, [40] but ignoring or breaking the laws of God would have the opposite effect. These laws of life and death apply equally to individuals, families, nations, and even civilizations.

> I call heaven and earth as witnesses today against you, that I have set before you life and death, blessing and cursing; therefore choose life, that both you and your descendants may live. Deuteronomy 30:19

God's eternal laws remain in force irrespective of people's belief systems. Just as with the Law of Gravity, it remains in force whether you believe it or not. If someone, for example, jumped out of an airplane, refusing to believe that the law of gravity exists, they would very quickly realize their error! Just as the Law of God leads to life, the rejection of God's law leads to death. It is eternally true that the wages or inevitable outcome of sin and rebellion against God are death. [41]

You cannot break the law of God; you can only break yourself upon it. (Dr. James Kennedy) [42]

Death is simply the absence of life. Because God is the author and sustainer of all life, it stands to reason that to separate oneself from God is to separate the individual or society from the source of life. When people turn away from God, their welfare is adversely affected; a truth abundantly illustrated throughout the ebb and flow of history. Previous generations understood these laws that have been ignored in the West today. When Hollywood producer and director Cecil B. DeMille made the first of two epic movies about the Ten Commandments in 1923, just a few years after the First World War, he made a statement about the importance of God's Law. As he explained at the beginning of his film, Mr. DeMille saw that the Great War was the direct result of the West abandoning the Law of God,

> Then through the laughter, came the shattering thunder of the World War. And now a blood-drenched, bitter world—no longer laughing—cries for a way out. Cecil B. DeMille, The Ten Commandments, 1923

With clear insight, this Hollywood mogul saw that civilization could not stand, apart from obeying God's higher law. Only God's Law can enable individuals and nations to live together in harmony. This same message is of vital importance today. The unfolding divisions and tensions internationally are evidence of the need for the West to return to its roots and foundations on the Word of God. Sadly, the long march of the Secularist Religion has well and truly overtaken all aspects of the entertainment industry that now preaches the secularism almost exclusively.

> The Ten Commandments are not rules to obey as a personal favor to God. They are the fundamental principles without which mankind cannot live together. They are not laws—they are the LAW. Cecil B. DeMille The Ten Commandments, 1923

People in the West, turning from the God who has proved himself so faithful over many centuries, now face the internal and external consequences. We must now face the inevitable consequences of arrogantly rejecting God and declaring Him obsolete. While the idea that God is dead has become an integral part of the pervasive secularist message, nothing could be further than the truth. It is not God who is dead, but rather the civilization that has rejected Him is dying. Erich Fromm (1900-1980) famously said, "In the nineteenth century, the problem was that God is dead. In the twentieth century, the problem is that man is dead."[43] If Fromm were alive today, I believe he would add, 'In the twenty-first century, the problem is that Western civilization is now dead.' If our civilization is not dead, it is at least sick and in its final death-throes. The West is now paying the ultimate price for abandoning its life-giving foundations. No, God is not dead; it's just that the West has lost its reason and gone mad. I recall Mark Twain's (1835-1910) words after an American newspaper reported his death when he said: "The report of my death was an exaggeration."[44]

> But why death? Death is God's limit on creatures whose sin is they want to be gods. We are not gods, and by death we learn that we are only human. Death is God's determination to limit our arrogance. D.A. Carson[45]

The West's cultural suicide

Suicide is abandoning our natural survival instincts and intentionally seeking death. Suicide cuts across our basic human disposition and is traditionally associated with psychological illness. Sometimes people with a terminal illness choose suicide to end their suffering, but those who are otherwise physically healthy sometimes decide that death is preferable to their lives.

Most people consider life precious, so suicide indicates a breakdown in logic or disconnect from reality—a psychological disorder. As a matter of observation, people often lose their desire to live when their dreams die, and their reason for living dies too. Whatever the reason, suicide is simply losing the will to live and wanting to end it all.

Apart from suicide, people also make lifestyle choices that adversely affect their health. It is a medical fact, for example, that activities such as smoking, over-eating, drug-taking, or excessive alcohol consumption can take years off a person's life expectancy. People are usually aware that these actions will harm their health but still choose them anyway. As a simile, whether through suicide or indulging practices harmful to health, Western civilization is also hastening its death.

> A country that is the product of Western civilization has a death wish when it sends billions of taxpayer dollars to a swag of fancy universities, few of which teach students the tenets of Western civilization.[46]

The deliberate attack on the West's foundations is a form of self-harm that is already producing sickness that will inevitably result in the death of Western society. The decline is still reversible at this time, and the adage 'where there's life, there's hope' comes to mind. However, if the West wants to damage its health and commit cultural suicide like the determined smoker, it surely will. Secularists believed that embracing materialism and rejecting God would create a new utopian society. Instead, the West had entered a new twilight zone of dystopia, reverting to the dark paganism that existed before the light of the Gospel dawned. Civilization gives way to barbarity, and without the unity of purpose leads to conflict and tribalism. Even secular commentators are aware of the implications of the West's departure from its foundations and the seriousness of the situation confronting it.

> In abandoning God, we are about to embark on one of the most radical social experiments in Western history. It is nothing short of the reordering of human nature. Short of war, nothing is as consequential.[47] Greg Sheridan

Without its traditional roadmap, the West is disordered. It cannot address its internal illness, let alone respond to the growing external threats from those who view democracy as inherently evil and seek its destruction. Western society seems to absorb the punches hoping it will all go away. However, unless it takes its internal and external threats seriously, the West will follow the Roman Empire's decline into oblivion. This chapter began by examining Oswald Spengler's view on the rise and fall of civilizations. The massive Roman Empire declined despite its superior weaponry, superior technology, organized public service, a system of law, and political sophistication. It collapsed when Alaric the Goth sacked Rome in 410 A.D. with a relatively inferior force. The decline and fall of Rome are well documented, but the consensus of historians is that it became rotten to the core and lost its resolve to exist. In modern language, it was so intent on keeping the party going that it lost its focus on everything else. Its moral decline meant it lacked the will to stand against a motivated enemy. In the end, it was collaborators within the city of Rome itself that opened the gates to its enemies. [48]

> There was also the great Roman Empire with its system of law, but there was a canker at the very heart of the Empire; and it finally collapsed, not because of the superior prowess of the Goths and the Vandals and the Barbarians, but because of the moral rot at its very heart. This was the cause of the 'decline and fall' of the great Roman Empire, as it is admitted by all. Dr. Martyn Lloyd-Jones.[49]

The new emerging geopolitical situation

While the prodigal West has been squandering its cultural inheritance, earned at high cost by previous generations, a new geopolitical reality is emerging in the East, challenging Western supremacy. While the West has been sleeping, the rest of the world has not. While the West is captivated by its narcissistic image in the gilded mirror of its delusions, the rest of the world looks on with disgust. Several eastern powers despise Western freedoms and are poised to challenge our pride and sense of entitlement. The current threats to the safety and stability of the West include militant Islam as embraced by Iran, North Korea, Russia, and most importantly of all, Communist China.

At some point, the West must wake up to its delusion and see the world as it is and not how it would like it to be. The reality is that the secularist revolution did not deliver the expected utopian outcomes it had hoped. Instead of world peace, the West is deeply divided, assailed by implacable foes representing a real and present danger. It must also wake up to see that the legalization of marijuana, thinking happy thoughts, and sending positive vibes at entertainment awards are not a prescription for world peace.

Without its traditional roadmap or game plan, the West finds it difficult to know what to do in the face of increased antagonism by those who seek to bring it down. So, it just keeps absorbing the blows of those who attack it, hoping it will all go away. Unless something changes, the West will follow the Roman Empire and the other great empires of history and decline into oblivion.

The last call for the prodigal West

Humanly speaking, the outlook for Western civilization is bleak. Having left the age of reason for one of confusion, its internal malaise has rendered it unable to confront its many implacable foes.

Having entered its winter phase, the West joins a long list of great civilizations that suffered decline and eventual death. At this point, there is still an available remedy, and that is to return to the roots and foundations that gave it life, direction, and identity. In every city, town, and hamlet in the Western world, churches bear witness to their allegiance to God in previous times. The obvious solution is to return to those things that previously gave it life and health. In the pendulum swing of history, this return to God has happened before, and it can happen again.

However, before the West can return to its spiritual and cultural roots, there must first be a revival of Jesus' message inside and outside the Church. We must appreciate the vast difference between God's amazing gift of love expressed in the Gospel and the external wrappings and cultural packaging of what has come to be known as Churchianity. This is the name coined to describe the institutional Church and its religious observances devoid of spiritual life.

It is man's self-effort and desire to build a society apart from God that is responsible for the evil things done in the name of religion down through the centuries. However, that is not because of the ineffectiveness of the Gospel to transform human nature and elevate societies and facilitate civilization—it is instead an indicator that Jesus' message has, in the past, been imperfectly implemented. As Victor Hugo, the author of The Hunchback of the Notre Dame and Les Misérables once said, "The holy law of Jesus Christ governs our civilization, but it does not yet permeate it"⁵⁰. Hugo recognized that the problem was not with the Gospel but with the fact that even in so-called Christian countries, people haven't taken His teaching seriously.

Just as the light of the Gospel shone brightest in the pagan darkness of the First Century Roman world, so too will the good news of God's love shine just as clearly in the deepest, darkest West when His Church returns to its spiritual roots. Whatever society's caricature of today's Church is, the idea of a world without God is infinitely worse.

Therefore, we should not reject Jesus' message but recognize the need for a more authentic expression of His teaching and its transforming power. For this reason, we urgently need revival and a new spiritual awakening today.

Instead of rejecting Jesus and His message, we need to learn how to allow His forgiveness, hope, and love to permeate our hearts, lives—and especially our society. Once we remove the ornate religious façade and cultural packaging of 'church,' we are left with a profound, precious reality that is in danger of being lost.

The story of the Prodigal Son recorded in Luke's Gospel (Luke 15:11-32) is a timeless parable that still speaks today. Parables are life stories with an eternal spiritual message. In this famous parable, Jesus told of a wayward son who had previously made terrible life choices but then learned from his mistakes and returned home to his father. The parable illustrates how individuals and society can turn things around when they wake up to their predicament and make the right choices.

The word prodigal is an old-school word that means to waste or misuse. In this insightful parable, Jesus' prodigal was a young man dazzled by the world's bright lights and then blew his inheritance on a party lifestyle. Thinking he will be better off, he leaves home to do his own thing. Having left home, this son of a wealthy landowner spectacularly trashed his life, spending his whole inheritance on partying and prostitutes (Luke 15:30). However, the party only lasted as long as his money did—and when it ran out, so did his so-called friends. Instead of the high life, he hit the wall financially and became homeless, lonely, and hungry.

Things were so bad that the only work he could find was tending a herd of pigs. The fact that pigs are non-kosher and forbidden only added to his humiliation and embarrassment as a good Jewish lad. The pay was so poor with this job on the pig farm that it left him continually hungry—he would gladly have eaten the pig food if he was allowed. Jesus said, 'he would gladly have filled his stomach with the pods that the swine ate, and no one gave him anything. Luke 15:16.'

One of the many timeless truths this parable teaches us is that valuable life lessons are sometimes learned through tough times, especially through our failures and bad decisions. Living with the pigs taught the prodigal truths that his father couldn't teach. The pig-slops were a powerful motivator for change and transformation.

It was only when the young man had spent everything he had and had hit the wall that then, and only then, he was able to see the severe consequences of his bad choices. Through his broken dreams and abject failure, he 'came to himself,'[51] woke up and remembered who he was. This awakening and self-awareness motivated him to return home to where he belonged. He was the son of a wealthy man, but he lived with pigs in a sty. This young man learned the hard way that he would continue to live like a hog and die like the proverbial dog unless he returned home.

Jesus' parable of the Prodigal Son offers insight to individuals and a society whose dreams have been shattered through blind delusions and bad decisions. The prodigal West has also squandered its cultural and spiritual inheritance to follow the fantasy of a romantic golden age apart from God. It, too, has lost its way, having been led astray by the bright lights of its utopian delusions. Thus, repentance and returning home are just as applicable to both the individual and our prodigal society. Just as Jesus' prodigal 'came to himself', Western civilization must also wake up to the reality of the rich heritage squandered by its rejection of God. Just as with Jesus' prodigal, what the father was unable to teach, is now being learned the hard way through the horrendous situation emerging in the West. If the pagan pig slops don't motivate a return home, perhaps the remembrance of former times will. The West must ask itself what is most important—home or the high life? What does it treasure? What matters most? And when it has answered these questions, it will be compelled to make some clear grown-up heart decisions.

> Like the prodigal son of the biblical parable, Western society has run away from God and wasted its inheritance—the Christian beliefs and ethics upon which our culture has been built over centuries. We now find ourselves lost, despairing, and hungry. Philip D. Jensen[52].

I recall the classic poem, The Hound of Heaven, by Francis Thompson (1859-1907) that is particularly applicable to the prodigal West these days. Although born into a prosperous middle-class family, Thompson rebelled and left home, became addicted to opium, and lived rough as a homeless person. Using the imagery of bloodhounds chasing their quarry, Thompson described himself in his poem as running away from God, despite knowing that He loved him. Like so many today, he was afraid that he would somehow miss out on the pleasures of life by following God.

> For though I knew His love who followed Yet was I sore adread, lest having Him, I should have nought beside. Francis Thompson (1859-1907)[53]

The poem climaxes with the heavenly pursuer catching up with this prodigal and the self-discovery that the very thing he was running from was what he needed most. All the benefits that enrich life, such as peace, love, and freedom, are found in Jesus. The thing that he was running from was what his soul required for fulfillment and completion.

'Ah, fondest, blindest, weakest, I am He Whom thou seekest!

Thompson came to see that he had made his bed in a hell of misery and dark despair. He had alienated himself from others and fled to the limits of loneliness, but he could not escape the pursuing love of God. So, may it be that the prodigal West experiences a similar awakening so that it too recognizes its need for God more than it can know.

PART THREE
TURNING THE TIDE

Four

THE LIGHT IS STILL SHINING

> I say that what we see in the cross is the glory of Godhead shining down upon us, first in the face of Jesus Christ.
> Martyn Lloyd-Jones [54]

Before Easter 2019, a fire destroyed the Notre Dame Cathedral in Paris. As this news reverberated worldwide, widespread expressions of grief and a deeply felt sense of loss ensued. These outpourings reflected not only the loss of this magnificent building but also the values and history it symbolized. The Cathedral represented a monument to a western civilization whose traditional foundations had been undermined, similarly in real danger of collapse. A newspaper headline reflected the mood of the moment; the banner reported, 'Civilization in Flames.' [55]

The fire that destroyed the Notre Dame Cathedral appears to have resulted from a tragic accident. By contrast, the destruction of the traditional fabric of Western civilization and culture has been deliberate. In both cases, however, something precious and irreplaceable has been lost—and only time will tell if their destruction is reversible. There are plans to rebuild the Cathedral, but the decline of the West continues unabated. People in the West now face the previously unthinkable prospect that its foundations are no longer sacrosanct. There is a possibility that its well-being is under threat, and its treasured liberal democracies may not survive.

There is an interesting sidebar to this story of the Notre Dame fire. Despite the destruction of the spire and roof, the altar remained intact, and so too its golden cross. Amazingly, its prayer candles were still burning. Each of these candles represented a prayer, reminding us that the fire could not extinguish the cry of the human heart as it calls out to God. Following the destructive fire, the light from these candles shone through the darkness.

The Cathedral's golden altar cross was seen standing as officials surveyed the charred structure. Votive candles lit prior to the blaze — each one symbolizing a prayer —still flickered undisturbed in the Cathedral, CNN reported. [56]

The light from heaven shining through the Cross

One of the standout images from the news coverage of the Notre Dame fire was the golden cross that gleamed through the smoke and haze of the burned-out building.[57] This image is a powerful metaphor, not only as a symbol of hope for the future but also for the spiritual awakenings that have occurred over the centuries, often at history's darkest times. Similarly, there have been many other times when it appeared the re-emerging pagan darkness would extinguish the light of the Gospel. However, the light from heaven has never stopped shining. In these dark times, God stepped down into history again and again in what was known as times of great awakening, and it was then that the Church received new life, and the community was blessed once more by the presence of God in the midst.

The Cross is the universally accepted symbol of the Christian faith, signifying salvation, hope, and love. Over two millennia ago, the message of the Cross ignited the most remarkable reset our world has seen, and today its truth is needed more than ever. The Cross reminds us of the pain and evil in our world and the pathway to goodness and salvation. It is the supreme and unmistakable testimony to the grace and love of God, and its message is the only hope that can save Western society from itself. Supremely the Cross reveals in unambiguous clarity the treatment of God's Son by a lost and confused world intent on pursuing its own agendas. It also attests to Jesus' resurrection from the grave to lead His people into rich fellowship with God and show them the way home to heaven.

The truth of Jesus' death and resurrection spread like a holy fire despite the persecution and opposition of succeeding Roman emperors. The power of the Gospel message was demonstrated by how it pierced the dark paganism of the Roman Empire. This light from heaven showed us how to live together in peace and love, and this reality provided the foundations of Western Civilization. The dynamic vitality and power of the Christian message were so great that within only a few generations, the Roman Emperor himself also became a follower of Jesus. The same light still shines, and the conquering power of God's love can still transform individual lives, families, societies, and even nations.

> The light shines through the darkness, and the darkness can never extinguish it. John 1:5 NLT

It is ironic that the Notre Dame Cathedral site previously hosted the worship of Jupiter, the Roman god of war. However, the message of God's forgiveness and the offer of peace with heaven drew people away from the pagan darkness by offering a completely different worldview. The love of Jesus replaced Jupiter's might-makes-right oppression and lust for power. If the burned-out Cathedral is a metaphor for the destruction of Western civilization, so too is the shining cross, an even more potent symbol for the light from heaven that can never be extinguished.

> This catastrophe in Paris today is a sign to all of us Christians, and a sign to all people in the West, especially those who despise the civilization that built this great temple to its God on an island in the Seine where religious rites have been celebrated since the days of pagan Rome. It is a sign of what we are losing, and what we will not recover, if we don't change course now. Dr. Guy Millière[58]

The Cross symbolizes the essence of the Christian message unadorned by the cultural wrapping of later centuries. Throughout 2,000 years of Church history, the Gospel message has been obscured by layers of human tradition. Instead of the spotlight falling on our Lord Jesus and His sacrifice for us, the Church has often seized center-stage, becoming a religious club to benefit its members and guests. When this happens, even sincere believers lose sight of the transformational, dynamic, revolutionary, and earth-shaking message preached by Jesus. Both inside and outside the Church, the West needs to desperately rediscover the vast difference between God's gift of love and its external packaging.

No one can deny the evil done in the name of religion down through the centuries. But, as previously stated, Victor Hugo recognized that the problem was not with Jesus' message but its inadequate implementation. What is needed is not the rejection of Jesus' message but a more authentic expression of His teaching and a renewed recognition of His transforming power. We urgently need another spiritual awakening that will restore the Church to the purity and life-changing power of the New Testament model.

Victor Hugo recognized that the problem was not with Jesus' message but its inadequate implementation

---

Instead of ignoring Jesus and His message, the West needs to understand that He is the only answer to our world's problems today. Heaven's peace plan is the only one that has ever worked. We need to relearn how to allow

His forgiveness, hope, and love to permeate our hearts, lives—and especially our society. Once the ornate religious façade and cultural packaging of 'church' are removed, the profound reality is precious.

For this reason, despite the spiritual tide being out, there are still millions of people in the West who faithfully gather for worship each week. So too, in the Middle East, where Christians are routinely persecuted for their faith, the Church is alive and growing. So too, in the Ukraine, where the population is under attack from an enemy force, believers pray and ask God's help to sustain them in these difficult times.

Following Jesus' birth, the dark times of history have been punctuated by visitations of the Holy Spirit, causing the Gospel light to shine brightly once again. These seasons of blessing are known as 'Great Awakenings', times when God stepped down into the affairs of men. These times of revival transformed individuals, communities, and even whole nations. This shining light from heaven produced the freedoms and social advances that Western culture so highly treasures.

> There, then, is the fact—that again and again in the history of the world, in the life of the Church, in the experience of the individual, **the darkest and most hopeless hours have preluded a new advent and invasion of the Spirit of God.** J.S. Stewart (1896-1990) [emphasis added]

It is highly significant that all major Christian denominations and movements were either born out of awakenings or have experienced a revival in their history. These awakenings ignited when God's people were brought to the place of brokenness and humility and began to cry out to God for his help.

Embracing truth and turning from darkness

Jesus came to reveal the truth about God and, just as importantly, the truth about man and his lost condition. He articulated an accurate diagnosis of humanity's status and then implemented salvation for a world dominated by man's selfish sinfulness. While human philosophies such as Marxism divide humanity into cohorts of oppressors and oppressed, the Gospel explains that society's problems are universal and affect everyone. As the apostle Paul stated, 'all have sinned and come short of the glory of God' (Romans 3:23).

> The breaking in of the truth about ourselves and about God, and the shattering of the illusion in which we have been living, is the beginning of revival for the Christian as it is of salvation for the lost.[59] Roy Hession (1908-1992)

When embracing the truth of the Gospel, individuals and societies can break the bondage of human nature. However, rejection of the Gospel truth causes a downward spiral towards moral and spiritual bankruptcy, as evident in our post-modern, post-truth twenty-first-century world. In his Epistle to the Romans, the Apostle Paul describes the decay of a society that has rejected God's truth; people 'suppress the truth of God by their wickedness' (Romans 1:18 NIV). Paul summarizes this rejection of truth with the succinct appraisal, 'professing to be wise they became fools' (Romans 1:22). By conscious rejection of the truth, Western civilization has 'exchanged the truth of God for a lie' (Romans 1:25 NIV). While there will be a future reckoning for rejection, God has allowed people to operate their free will for the present time. The Bible says, 'God gave them up' (Romans 1:24). The generations who have chosen to forsake God have now become God-forsaken.

As people struggle to discern truth from fake news and delusion in our modern world, it is encouraging to know that the light from heaven is still shining. Our daily news services remind us of the dark confusion enveloping our planet and the challenges that confront us, for which there is no human solution. However, experience teaches us that lamenting or even cursing the darkness will change nothing. Instead, we must embrace the light of truth and allow this to guide us. Jesus is the Light of the World, and we desperately need His light more than ever. The great truths of the Gospel are just as powerful as they were when they pierced the darkness of the first-century Roman world. God's divine love is still the beacon of hope to the whole human race, and this light will lead us home.

Jesus is the living embodiment of truth

Jesus Christ didn't only speak the truth; He was also the living embodiment and concrete reality, truth incarnated in human form. When He was on trial before a Roman tribunal, He didn't seek to defend Himself against trumped-up charges but declared that he had come to bear witness to THE truth. Jesus was on trial before Pontius Pilate, the Roman governor, a representative of the Roman Caesar who thought he was a god. Jesus was on trial for his life, but in reality, the whole world was also on trial for its ultimate treatment of the Son of God, whose only crime was that He both told and lived out the truth of God.

When Jesus, the Light of the World, came to planet earth, He confronted the delusions and confusion of a lost world. The truth of the Gospel confronted dark paganism, setting people free. The pagan gods exercised power only because they deluded their victims. By contrast, Heaven's light testifies to the truth of the Cross. The Cross reveals the love of God and the emptiness of man, and finally shows the way home for lost humanity.

- The Cross shines forth the love of God
- The Cross reveals the truth of man's fatal flaw
- The Cross shows us the way home

The Cross shines out the truth of God's love

Jesus' sacrifice on the Cross is the supreme demonstration of God's love. This death is at the center of the Gospel. It reveals the heart of God and resonates deeply with the human condition. The apostle Paul and others later discovered that Jesus didn't only die for His friends but also for those who hated Him and wanted Him dead. Jesus didn't just talk about love; He demonstrated it. His passion, shining through the pagan world, ignited a revolution of peace and love.

The light from the Cross reveals to the whole world the true nature of God, as embodied in Jesus Christ. The West has rejected its Christian foundations mainly because it is totally in the dark about who Jesus is. By missing this vital truth, they have embraced a caricature, ignoring reality. When someone tells me that they don't accept that there is a God, this arouses my interest. I ask them to define the God in whom they don't believe. In almost every case, they describe a spiteful, vengeful god with no concern for their welfare who is only interested in making their lives miserable. This pagan view of God was famously expressed by William Shakespeare in King Lear: 'As flies to wanton boys are we to th' gods. They kill us for their sport.' That is not the God of the Bible, but a pagan view stitched together in the minds of ignorant men.

The Light of the World came to set the record straight, penetrating darkness and confusion. Then, as now, God's message from heaven to our skeptical world is 'love your neighbor as yourself'.

> Jesus didn't love us because we are special; we are special because we are loved. Bishop Festo Kivengere.

The message of the Cross leaves no doubt about the love of God for our world; it is black and white, leaving no grounds for conjecture. We must either accept or reject the light of God's love. Jesus taught His disciples that there is no greater love than for a man to lay down his life for his friends (John 15:13). This universal truth resonates deeply across cultural and ethnic divides and goes to the heart of our humanity.

History is peppered with people who vehemently opposed the Gospel but subsequently decided to follow Jesus when they comprehended His love for them. The apostle Paul was initially one of the most vehement opponents of the Gospel, going so far as to sanction the murder of Stephen. He was defending the Law of Moses against what he saw as the challenge from the teachings of Jesus. However, once God opened Paul's eyes, he saw that Jesus was love incarnate and the fulfillment of God's law. The Ten Commandments provided a roadmap to life and pointed the way to man's supreme welfare; Jesus came to interpret and embody all that the law stipulated. Love is the fulfillment of the law, and Jesus demonstrated God's divine love profoundly and unmistakably.

The most vicious, God-hating demon from hell cannot erase the truths about God, as demonstrated by the Cross. God loved the world so much that He gave his only begotten Son that whosoever believes in him should not perish but have everlasting life (John 3:16). Skeptics have the God-given gift of free will to reject Him, but they cannot erase God's love for them. Their rejection of Jesus merely shows the darkness of their own heart for which they will one day give an account to God.

The Cross shines forth the truth of man's fatal flaw

> Not only does the Cross of Jesus shine forth the truth of God's love, but it also vividly displays the true nature of man in that we crucified the Lord of glory. When the news of Jesus' resurrection circulated on the Day of Pentecost, the apostle Peter proclaimed that 'you killed Him, but God raised Him up' (Acts 2:23-24).

The rejection of the Son of God through the ages clearly illustrates an ugly truth that secularists are unwilling to acknowledge—the reality of man's fatal moral defect. When push comes to shove, human nature will choose what it thinks will be of personal benefit over what it knows to be right. This is where Secularist Religion stands in fierce opposition to the Gospel of Jesus

Christ. Secularists believe in the fundamental goodness of man, who only needs to make political adjustments to save himself from the evils of society. The Gospel asserts that man can't save himself and needs a Savior. The Cross exposes the true nature of sinful man. He rejected, tortured, and crucified the spotless Son of God to maintain his darkness. The truth is that despite their high aspirations, apart from cultural and legal restraints, individual human beings will (with very few exceptions) always act in self-interest and put themselves before the interests of others. Jesus died to address this very issue. This same selfish motivation underpins the West forsaking its spiritual and cultural heritage by turning away from following Jesus in our day.

The apostle Paul was highly religious even before becoming a Christian, strictly adhering to his Jewish religion's code of practice. However, looking back, Paul was compelled to face something that none of us wants to confront; his grave character flaw. Despite having an education in the classics on top of his advanced religious training, Paul conceded that he didn't understand his inner motives because his behavior baffled him. 'What I choose and intend to do, I don't implement and carry out. By contrast, those things that I really hate to do, I end up doing' (Romans 7:15).

Secularism mounts the argument that doing the right thing is rational and reasonable, and people will make the right choices without any moral imperative from religion or God. However, our daily news sources are full of stories that involve intelligent, well-educated people misbehaving. The apostle Paul discovered through personal experience what millions of people throughout history have found; the crass complexity of human nature. Intelligent and otherwise successful people sometimes act like fools and seek to excuse their indefensible activities when their behavior is exposed. This fatal flaw motivated countries like Nazi Germany to go to war, believing it would lead to a better future. It is also why nations with nuclear capabilities like Iran, North Korea, Russia, and China throw their weight around and bully other countries. It makes no sense. Everyone will be a loser in a nuclear war, but it seems not to affect their belligerent behavior. Jesus is the Savior of the world and our only hope.

> The fall was putting "I" as the center of life, and redemption is putting man back to the center of love, which is "not I". FB Meyer (1847-1929) [60]

The Cross shines the truth on man's way home

When Jesus was born, angelic messengers proclaimed, 'peace on earth and goodwill towards men'. His mission was to effect the reconciliation of humanity to God by removing every barrier. The Cross of Jesus is heaven's bold declaration that Jesus demolished every impediment to man's reconciliation with God, the first step in our journey to our heavenly home. Just as the Cross is an undeniable witness to God's love, so it is also a stark reminder of the payment of our redemption price. Man is forgiven—his fatal flaw overcome.

This truth is so simple that a child can understand it, yet so profound that the great minds of history have been unable to plumb its depths. The good news of the Gospel is that Jesus conquered the grave and showed us the way to eternal life in heaven. The way to heaven is through turning from our rebellion and putting our trust in Jesus Christ as our only Savior.

The indictment of the Cross

We have already noted that the Cross is the universally accepted symbol of the Christian faith and a distillation of the central truth of the Gospel. Its appeal is universal in that it speaks to people from every ethnic group and demographic—rich or poor, young or old. Significantly, at His crucifixion, Jesus' alleged crimes were listed in Greek, Latin, and Hebrew so that everyone would understand the charges against Him.

The notice publicized that Jesus wasn't killed by a lynch mob but by a legally convened Roman tribunal. The charges against Jesus confirmed that He died for speaking the truth to a deluded world. Jesus died at the 'place of the skull', now known as Calvary. Following standard Roman legal practice, a list of His 'crimes' was nailed to His Cross for all to see.

> And an inscription also was written over Him in letters of Greek, Latin, and Hebrew: THIS IS THE KING OF THE JEWS. Luke 23:38

The Cross and the indictment of Jesus graphically portray humanity's response to God's gift of a Savior. When it came time to choose, they opted to release a robber and crucify Jesus. Thus, Jesus was rejected and brutalized by a world that resented heaven's peace offer and preferred its power structures. As the prophet Isaiah foretold, Jesus was 'despised and rejected by men.' It is a sad fact of human nature that we often prefer our contrived delusions to the reality of our lost condition. We not only build castles in the air but demand the right to live in them. The integrity of the Cross supremely shines the light of heaven's truth on the spiritual emptiness of the whole human race.

Before condemning Jesus to death, Pontius Pilate recognized Jesus' trial for what it was—a politically motivated travesty of justice. Pilate hoped that having Jesus flogged would satisfy the bloodlust of the crowd. But even after Jesus' heinous flogging, they still petitioned for His death. Before his crucifixion, Jesus was inhumanely humiliated and ridiculed. He was flogged with a flagellum, similar to a cat-o'-nine-tails. He was then stripped naked, slandered, and cursed by soldiers. They forced a crown of thorns upon His head and dressed him in the mock robes of an emperor. Regaled with the crown and purple robes, they spat on and ridiculed Him, saying: 'hail king of the Jews'. This extreme abuse took place before they forced Him to carry His Cross to the site of execution.

The sign on Jesus' Cross left no doubt about what occurred that day. The society of Jesus' time was a confluence of three great cultures, representing the pinnacle of human achievement in philosophy, law, and religion, so Jesus' indictment spoke clearly to the Greek, Roman, and Jewish worlds. Moreover, John's Gospel records that no one could miss the impact of Calvary. His execution took place out in the open, in a public space, 'near the city.' [61] The charges were clear for all to see so that no one could avoid the significance of this moment in history.

The indictment against Jesus was written in Latin.

Latin was the language of the Romans, who had established an empire by force of arms. Their empire extended throughout the Mediterranean world and into Europe. On top of their military might and technological advancements, the Romans prided themselves in their legal system. It is a testimony to their achievements that Latin was the language of science and learning for centuries. Latin words and definitions appear extensively in our legal language today. It was an indictment of the Roman legal system that their language listed the charges on Jesus' Cross. They acknowledged that they had knowingly condemned an innocent man to death. Jesus, innocent of all charges, was murdered for political expediency and not because of the demands of justice. When Pilate questioned Jesus, he found Him blameless but ordered His executed anyway—a complete travesty of justice from any perspective.

The indictment against Jesus was written in Greek.

The ancient Greeks were renowned for their elevation of reason and their pursuit of wisdom. They wrote the book on philosophy, and even the word 'philosophy' is a Greek compound that describes their love of wisdom. Greek was still the language of classical learning in the first-century world. Hence the New Testament was written for posterity in this language. Even today, we study the ancient Greek philosophers, with their classic writings influencing Western culture for centuries. When Jesus' indictment was written in Greek, it only illustrated their flawed reasoning. They were astute and should never have rejected the Son of God. God created us all with an intellect, but the Greeks missed the spiritual dimension by relying on pure reason. Their intelligence never enabled them to find God, and the idea of a crucified Savior was irrational. They understood the concept of logos as the mind behind the universe, but the indictment written in Greek shows that when the 'Word (logos) became flesh', their wisdom and logic had failed them.

The indictment against Jesus was also written in Hebrew.

Hebrew was the language of the Jewish people; they wrote their Old Testament in this ancient language. Judaism represented the ultimate religion, handed down by God through Moses. Despite the Jewish people having no homeland for nearly 2000 years, the Hebrew language miraculously survived, springing back to life with the birth of the modern state of Israel in 1948. Hebrew was declared their official language when the Jewish people were granted their homeland through a United Nations charter.

The charges against Jesus were written in the Hebrew language, and this was an indictment against their empty religion. In practical terms, they rejected and then crucified the son of God—the very One they claimed to worship. But they had no excuse. The ancient prophecies concerning the Jewish messiah were clear and unmistakable; the Jewish leaders knew that Jesus came from God. But that didn't prevent their religious machinations and decision to kill him.

Nicodemus was a member of the Jewish Sanhedrin and later declared his faith in Jesus. He took a stand with Joseph of Arimathea by helping prepare Jesus' body for burial.[62] When Nicodemus first came in secret to ask questions about Jesus' teaching, he made it clear that the Jewish leaders knew that He had come from God. But they still crucified Him. Their instinct for political survival and commitment to the religious system eclipsed their moral judgment to do what they knew to be right. And right there is the failure of religion in every age.

> Religion is man's attempt to reach up to find God. The Gospel of Jesus is about God reaching down to help man. The Cross bears clear testimony to the failure of human attempts at religion. Man's fatal flaw means that all manufactured religion is doomed to fail, which is why Jesus had to come and save us from ourselves.

Only when we understand the failure of all of man's best efforts in law, philosophy, and religion will we see how lost our humanity is and how much we need a savior. When we understand the love of God and the lost predicament of man, then it is we realize that Jesus is our only hope.

The Cross emphasizes the love of God and the true nature of man. Discovering these truths, we can choose to turn to the light and accept Jesus as our Lord and Savior. It is a simple choice that completely changes our destiny. This truth ignited the first Gospel revolution, and this same truth is still shining into our world today. The darkness can never extinguish the light of the Gospel. Western culture's rejection of Jesus and his Gospel indicates man's obvious fatal flaw. We urgently need an awakening to this truth and a new turning to Jesus today.

Five

THE AWAKENINGS OF THE PAST

> Revival is the visitation of God which brings to life Christians who have been sleeping and restores a deep sense of God's near presence and holiness. Thence springs a vivid sense of sin and a profound exercise of heart in repentance, praise, and love, with an evangelistic outflow. J.I. Packer (1926-2020)[63]

What is an awakening?

There have been times when God stepped down into human history and directly intervened in the affairs of men. His purpose always was to fulfill His plans for humanity, plans that He had determined before creating the world. Historians commonly refer to these interventions as the 'Great Awakenings'.

> The significance of these awakenings is that the prayers of His people always ignited them.
> Always.

People that have experienced the revivals caused by these awakenings have left us a record of their gestation, and we can learn from this. Historically, in addition to the Reformation, there have been three Great Awakenings in Church history, known as the First, Second, and Third Great Awakenings. Some scholars also include other revivals and movements in this list, but I will concentrate on these three.

There is confusion, even amongst believers, regarding the difference between revivals and awakenings. There also seems to be significant disagreement about whether we can expect another awakening today. Various groups use different terminology to describe a 'move of God' or a 'revival' or an 'awakening.' These explain how the Lord impacts churches and society in unusual ways. However, the word revival describes new spiritual life experienced either by an individual or a church brought into a closer relationship with Jesus. By contrast, the word awakening describes a much broader impact when God steps down to visit his people and results in the reformation of the entire society.

> The words "revival" and "awakening" are often used interchangeably, but there is a distinction. **An awakening takes place when God sovereignly pours out his Spirit, and it impacts a culture.** That is what happened during the Jesus Revolution, and it's what happened in multiple spiritual awakenings in the history of the United States, predating its establishment as a nation.[64] Greg Laurie [Emphasis added]

The history of past awakenings illustrates how God has often stepped down into man's affairs to impact and transform individual lives and whole communities. These awakenings affected their contemporary societies to such an extent that they changed the direction of history. Those within and outside the Church recognized the phenomenon, and even secular historians acknowledged and recorded their impact. Despite the different views about awakenings, there is a general agreement about those called 'great'—the First, Second, and Third Great Awakenings. Others include the Welsh Revival and the Jesus Movement of the 1970s and '80s as significant Awakenings. There is no doubt that these moves of God both had considerable influence on Western culture. Robert J. Morgan accepts this view in his insightful article in the Huffington Post titled, The Sixth Great Awakening: America's Only Hope.

Another feature of the past awakenings is that they often happened in some of history's darkest times. The First and Second Great Awakenings, for example, burst on the scene after generations of spiritual and social decay. One could argue that this decline first motivated people inside and outside the Church to call on God for his help. Thus, history teaches us that the significant social advances of the past weren't the result of social evolution but rather the turning of the moral tide resulting from God's divine intervention.

As an example of how the Lord often moves during history's darkest times, the First Great Awakening exploded among students in Oxford University in the 1730s. At that time, skepticism in the academic community was rife, resulting in a falling away from faith and belief in God. This rejection of God resulted in widespread social and moral disintegration. Consequently, the awakening shook Britain and then the American colonies to the core as people, in the tens of thousands, flocked to hear the good news of Jesus.

For the first time, people heard the message of God's salvation and love, unadorned by that day's cultural and religious packaging.

> First came the Great Awakening, which dates to around 1740. The writings of the French skeptics and the Enlightenment thinkers so pervaded the Colonies that churches struggled to remain open. Colleges became hotbeds of humanism, and Christian students, what few there were, practiced their faith secretly. Robert J. Morgan[65]

Similar scenes accompanied the Second Great Awakening, which was birthed in the late Eighteenth but burst into flames in the early Nineteenth Century. Before this awakening, the Church was dead, formal, and morally bankrupt from top to bottom. In both cases, skeptics said, 'we don't believe in God', then God decided to move.

> The prevalence of wickedness is no evidence at all that there is not going to be a revival. That is often God's time to work. When the enemy cometh in like a flood, the Spirit of the Lord lifts up a standard against him. Charles Finney.[66] (1792-1875)

These first two awakenings impacted their respective communities in such a way as to seismically shake both Great Britain as well as its American colonies. It was as though God was saying to those who chose not to believe in God, 'here I am—ready or not!' For this reason, I am confident of seeing another awakening in our day. The spiritual tide has been well and truly out for decades, and Western society is now beginning to reap what it sowed by its rejection of God. In the Biblical record and the history of the Church, the present darkness is a powerful motivator for people to seek God and pursue the light. The almost universal declaration by the Western intelligentsia is that God is dead, but theirs is not the final word on the subject. Just as in previous awakenings, God may yet show up and say, 'Here is my response to your theories—deal with it!'

Christian leaders have been talking about the need for revival and awakening for some years. Still, only now are believers waking up to the peril they face from persecution and marginalization by Secularist Religion. Only now is a sense of desperation being translated into fervent, heartfelt prayer. Our heavenly Father has promised to answer such prayers, and that will change everything.

What happens in times of awakening?

When God brings revival, we see a clear pattern emerge as He steps down into human history. The following list is not exhaustive, but it does provide some guidelines from the past to show what took place after God's people humbled themselves to pray and cry out for His help.

The manifest presence of God

One of the outstanding features of awakenings is that when God steps down, His presence feels very close and tangible. For the believer walking with the Lord, He always seems close, but His presence is magnified in the Church and community in times of awakening. Those who have experienced a past revival call this phenomenon of God's nearness the manifest presence of God. The Lord is always present with His people, but His reality is often manifested in unique ways in times of awakening.

> Both Old and New Testaments record instances where the invisible God manifested His presence visibly, audibly or with other supernatural signs. We read, for example, how the Lord manifested His presence at Mount Sinai, covering the mountain in smoke as 'the LORD descended upon it in fire' (Exodus 19:18).

On the Day of Pentecost, God's power and presence overshadowed the birth of the Church. At the end of Jesus' earthly ministry, He left only 120 followers meeting together after His resurrection to pray for the Holy Spirit to come (Acts 1:14). After praying for The Promise of the Father for ten days, the Holy Spirit descended on this small group of believers. Jesus Christ had conquered the grave and was then present with His people, impacting the whole of Jerusalem. Even those who had crucified Jesus only seven weeks earlier had to conclude that Jesus had indeed risen from the grave. Confronted by the presence of God in their midst, 3,000 people swept into the Kingdom on the Day of Pentecost alone.

It wasn't sound doctrine or heartfelt worship that impacted the crowds visiting Jerusalem for the Feast of Pentecost. Instead, the first-century world was staggered by the presence of God among his people, a reality saturated with His divine love.

Some aspects of the Holy Spirit on the day of Pentecost were unique to the occasion. But other features have been repeated during later awakenings.

For example, visible tongues of fire and audible sounds of a mighty wind were not a subsequent widespread phenomenon. However, God's overwhelming presence has been a feature of awakenings down the centuries.

An example of the manifest presence of God involved Jonathan Edwards (1703-1758), a pastor in Northampton, Massachusetts, during the First Great Awakening. This Christian minister was a rather serious Calvinist who reportedly read his sermons in a dull monotone, word by word, from his notes. However, when God visited Jonathan Edwards' community, everyone outside and inside the Church knew about it. Writing about this visitation of God later, Jonathan Edwards describes how in 1735, the whole town seemed to be full of God's presence.[67]

In times of awakening, believers and whole communities experienced the manifest presence of God; everyone could see evidence of God at work. That same sense of God's presence appeared in the eyewitness accounts of a more localized revival in Scotland soon after World War II. In what became known as the Hebrides Revival of 1949-1952, there was an outpouring of the Holy Spirit in response to the prayers of God's people. When the revival broke out, a sense of God's presence gripped their meetings, and there was an overflow of blessing into the community. As God visited His Church, there were also manifestations of His presence in the lives of non-attenders. His presence became a reality to many opposed to the Gospel. Although against the revival all around them, they were gripped by the need to get right with God. All eyewitness accounts reported this same story of God's presence infecting the Church and community. Owen Murphy, who wrote an eyewitness account of the Hebrides revival titled, When God Stepped Down from Heaven, wrote:

> Revival is an "awareness of God" that grips the whole community, and the roadside, the tavern, as well as the church, becomes the place where men find Christ. Here is the vast difference between our modern evangelistic campaigns and true revival. In the former, hundreds may be brought to a knowledge of Christ, and churches experience seasons of blessings but as far as the community is concerned little impact is made; the taverns, dance halls, and movies are still crowded, and godlessness marches on. In revival, the Spirit of God like a cleansing flame sweeps through the community. Divine conviction grips people everywhere; the strongholds of the devil tremble and many close their doors, while multitudes turn to Christ! [68]

A fresh revelation of Jesus

The arrival of Jesus Christ was the central message of the early Church, focusing on the One who had died on the Cross and rose from the grave victorious. The Gospel is about the Light shining from heaven, enabling people to see that Jesus Christ is the Son of God. This was not about blind faith in His post-resurrection meeting with His disciples; Jesus demonstrated His authority and power by 'presenting Himself alive after His sufferings' (Acts 1:3). Unfortunately, there has been a tendency down the ages to reduce the Gospel to a formula, or even worse, a matter of mere religious observance based on human effort. The Church that Jesus built understood that the foundation of their faith centered on Jesus and their relationship with Him.

> Seeing Him we are convicted of sin, broken, cleansed, filled with the Spirit, set free from bondage, and revived. Each aspect of Christian experience is made real in us just by seeing Him.
> Roy Hession (1908-1992) [69]

Saul of Tarsus, later known as the apostle Paul, encountered Jesus, transforming his life. Not all encounters with Jesus are as dramatic as Paul's, but whether through the Word of God or the testimony of others, the Christian life begins with the recognition of the reality of Jesus Christ. Paul was an opponent of the Gospel but became a follower of Jesus through encountering the risen Savior on the Damascus Road. Jesus had been publicly executed and rose from the grave, so Paul's encounter meant he would never be the same again. Paul was religious and zealously defended the traditions and teachings of his ancestors. Paul was never able to get over that, despite deserving God's judgment for persecuting the Church, Jesus forgave him and manifested His love, grace, and forgiveness to one who saw himself as the chief of sinners.[70]

As well as our five physical senses, the Bible teaches that each human being also has a spiritual dimension by which we may comprehend the unseen spiritual world. We can know about Jesus intellectually through the usual human senses but still not understand Him as the Savior of the world. From a human perspective, Jesus is often viewed as a good man, perhaps a prophet or a moral teacher or some such. But, seen from God's perspective, He is so much more. In times of spiritual awakenings, people's spiritual eyes perceive Jesus as He is, a divine friend, helper, and the only one who can save us from ourselves.

In times of revival, those inside the Church suddenly see Jesus in a new light. Outsiders get converted to follow Him. In the mid-twentieth century, William Ngenda was a leader in the East African revival and later proclaimed the revival message to Western churches. To those who held unbiblical expectations of revival, Mr. Ngenda declared that 'Revival is having our spiritual eyes opened to see Jesus.'[71]

We see this illustrated in the life of the prophet Isaiah. He was a prophet of God who proclaimed miseries against his contemporaries, as recorded in the book that carries his name. However, everything changed when he received a fresh vision of God in His Temple. His spiritual eyes opened to see the glory of God, revealing his abject poverty of spirit. Isaiah's experience prompted the apostle Paul to pray for believers at Ephesus, asking God to open their spiritual eyes to see Jesus. He wanted them to recognize His working in their lives.

Charles Finney (1792-1875), an evangelist and revivalist in the 19th century, testified to a personal encounter with Jesus soon after giving his life to Him. Finney had a vision of Jesus where His love and immediacy became real. Wherever Finney went, revivals followed as the presence of Jesus in Finney's life became apparent to everyone. This is the pattern we see repeatedly recurring in the great awakenings in history.

> As I went in and shut the door after me, it seemed as if I met the Lord Jesus Christ face to face.... He said nothing, but looked at me in such a manner as to break me right down at His feet. I wept aloud like a child, and made such confessions as I could with my choked utterance." ... "As I turned and was about to take a seat by the fire, I received a mighty baptism of the Holy Ghost.... No words can express the wonderful love that was shed abroad in my heart. I wept with joy and love.[72]

It is unclear whether Mr. Finney's experience was an external vision or an internal impression. Few people see external visions of Jesus like Mr. Finney, but He makes Himself real, nonetheless. The Bible teaches that our spiritual eyes and ears are an essential part of our humanity, and by them, we can detect Jesus' presence. In addition to historical examples, I have heard countless testimonies by people who were awakened to see Jesus differently. Although no two experiences are the same, Jesus still becomes more real.

Sometimes people think about God when they fall in love or bear their first child. Often, they experience hopeless situations and call out to God for help. Regardless of how people awaken, it is always a work of the Holy Spirit. Many people testify that the rituals associated with 'doing church' obscure the reality of the Gospel.

> God's gift can be hidden by cultural wrapping paper, which conceals the light. In times of awakening, however, it's as though the wrappings disappear, and the veil is swept aside so they can see Jesus as He is.

John Wesley's (1703-1792) conversion illustrates how a professional clergyman can be blind to the truth of the Gospel. His conversion and subsequent ministry are incredible stories of spiritual awakening in Church history. Like the apostle Paul, Wesley had an impressive religious pedigree, but his encounter with Jesus transformed his life.

Wesley was a minister's son before training for the ministry at Oxford University. Later he was a tutor at Oxford and earned a master's degree, then traveled to the US colony of Georgia as a missionary. Wesley's ship sailed into a storm during his Atlantic crossing and looked like it would sink. Wesley realized that even though he was a Church leader, he didn't know Jesus personally. After failing miserably in Georgia, he returned to London. In a house meeting, his spiritual eyes opened to see Jesus. He later recorded in his diary that his heart was "strangely warmed" as Jesus became real to him.[73] When he personally experienced God's love and forgiveness, a holy fire ignited in his heart. His religious zeal was too much for some of his contemporaries. Doors closed, preventing him from preaching in Anglican churches. Since he was unable to proclaim his holy fire in buildings or institutions, he preached in fields and public areas throughout the length and breadth of Britain. Again, Wesley was brought up in the Church and had received a theological education before he awoke to know Jesus personally.

The transformation of society

Over the last 50 years, secularists have tried to explain Western Civilization's progress as cultural and social evolution. Unfortunately, secularists, and many believers, do not appreciate the significant, positive contributions of past great awakenings. The social advances in Western culture did not emanate from the Enlightenment but were the direct result of the various awakenings. These awakenings brought communities and nations back to the foundational truths on which they were originally established.

History reveals that the great awakenings were preceded by moral decadence and social disintegration. However, when the light of the Gospel began to shine, societies were healed, revived, and flourished once more. This is especially true of the Second Great Awakening, which had such a profound positive impact on Western civilization and whose effects are still evident today.

In the late 18th century, society in England was in dire straits. The land reforms and Enclosure Acts forced people off the land and into the towns and cities. This migration later provided the workforce for the Industrial Revolution, accompanied by a new range of challenges. The destructive impact on people's moral and spiritual well-being was catastrophic. With the loss of family and community cohesion, towns and cities became breeding grounds for sickness vice and crime.

> The French traveler and mathematician La Condamine said that he had visited the most barbarous cities in the world (he instanced Russia, Turkey, Algiers, Tunis, Tripoli, Morocco, and Egypt), and had never seen savages to equal Londoners. In his view, the inhabitants of the Capital were more ferocious and fearsome than any other group of people from China to Peru.[74]

In tandem with social decline, the spiritual life of the Church was at a low ebb and slowly dying. Influenced by Deism, which viewed Christianity as a set of rules, the growth of atheism closed people's eyes to God. As a result, English and American societies were strongly affected by anti-Christian skepticism and the lawlessness that went with it.

> After the Revolutionary War, Christianity lapsed into another decline as large numbers of Americans pressed into unchurched territories west of the Appalachians. In the East, too, the work of the Lord declined as people busied themselves with building a new nation. By the 1790s, only one in 10 Americans attended worship. Chief Justice John Marshall told Bishop Madison, "The church is too far gone ever to be redeemed." Voltaire said, "In 30 years' time Christianity will be forgotten." Voltaire's disciple in America, Thomas Paine, wrote, "Of all the systems of religion that were ever invented, there is nothing more

derogatory to the Almighty, more unedifying to man, more repugnant to reason, and more contradictory in itself, than this thing called Christianity.[75] Robert J. Morgan

If the First Great Awakening resulted in new life in the Church, the Second Great Awakening began to transform society radically. As people started to see Jesus in a new light, they turned from selfish sinfulness to being concerned about the welfare of others. The light of the Gospel penetrated this world of darkness where the masses wallowed in poverty, sin, and misery. And just as in the First Great Awakening, both rich and poor received the Gospel message with gratitude.

> As people started to see Jesus in a new light, they turned from selfish sinfulness to being concerned about the welfare of others. The light of the Gospel penetrated this world of darkness where the masses wallowed in poverty, sin, and misery

---

It is impossible to adequately describe the social transformation that began with the Second Great Awakening. Its influence continued throughout the 19th century and led to the Third Great Awakening. Concern for social justice motivated a raft of reforms that we take for granted today.

The Sunday school movement began in Britain in the 1780s when the Industrial Revolution resulted in many children working full time in factories. They aimed to teach children literacy and provide skills to end the poverty cycle. Robert Raikes (1725-1811), an evangelical Anglican, championed this cause, motivating other Christian philanthropists to battle the exploitations of child labor. In the 1800s, laws were introduced to reduce the number of hours children worked to 12, and other reforms to stop the exploitation of children followed. In addition, Methodist laymen fought for social justice in the adult workplace. These committed Christians began trade unions to stand against the exploitation of greedy employers long before Marx published Das Kapital in 1867. In 1834 a group who became known as the Tolpuddle Martyrs were arrested on trumped-up charges and sentenced to deportation to the Australian Colonies. These men were commonly recognized as the first pioneers of trade unionism, whereas today, unions are generally involved in advancing the Socialist cause.

> The Tolpuddle Martyrs, especially the Loveless brothers and Thomas Standfield, were very clear that their lives were dedicated to serving God, as committed Christians in the Methodist tradition. It influenced all areas of their life, including work, what they read and wrote, and how they behaved at all times.[76]

This same wave of Christian love produced by the Second Great Awakening led to the establishment of schools, food distribution to the poor, prison reforms, and perhaps most famously, the abolition of slavery. William Wilberforce (1759-1833), a young Member of Parliament, led the fight against slavery after converting to faith in Jesus. He was influenced by John Newton (1725-1807), a colorful preacher in London who had previously lived a godless life as a sailing captain involved in the African slave trade. Newton is best known as the author of Amazing Grace, arguably the best-known hymn of all time. Newton encouraged Wilberforce to serve the Lord in parliament, where he introduced a bill for the abolition of slavery. He campaigned for years until the Slavery Abolition Act finally passed in 1833. Wilberforce was also active in other social reforms, including the RSPCA (Royal Society for the Prevention of Cruelty to Animals) and the Royal National Lifeboat Institution. In another lesser-known project, Wilberforce and others tackled alcohol abuse problems. They tried to steer people away from drinking gin in favor of beer, which was less potent and harmful.

The Second Great Awakening also ignited the Modern Missionary Movement. Just as the first century Roman Peace (Pax Romana) facilitated the initial spread of the Gospel, the technological advances of the 19th century, including travel and communication, promoted widespread exposure to the Gospel. In addition, foreign trade provided routes into lands previously inaccessible.

In later years the motives of pioneer missionaries were frequently vilified or twisted. However, the biographies of missionaries from William Carey onwards reveal stories of sacrificial service and powerful transformation of lives as people embraced the good news of Jesus. Despite some failures, there were also incredible successes as the Gospel penetrated India, Africa, China, and the South Seas, usually at significant personal cost. I recall, for example, a visit to a cultural center in Fiji when the guide explained that before the Gospel transformed their people and nation, the Fijians were cannibals and headhunters. Today, they are known as being amongst the friendliest people on earth.

During the Welsh Revival of 1904-1905, a social revolution occurred when multitudes flocked to hear the Gospel. This revival spread throughout the Principality of Wales and transformed the nation. The Gospel straightened out lives, marriages and families restored, and many turned away from alcohol abuse. Countless stories relate how the crime rate dropped to a point where the police had nothing to do except control the crowds thronging the churches. One eyewitness, Jesse Penn-Lewis, who also knew many of the revival's leaders, personally recorded the revival up close.

> Long-standing debts were paid. Stolen goods returned. Prizefighters, gamblers, publicans, rabbit-coursers, and others of the class rarely touched by ordinary means came to Christ, and quickly the world knew the results. Magistrates were presented with white gloves in several places because there were "no cases." Public houses were forsaken. Rowdiness was changed to soberness. Oaths ceased to be heard, so that, it was said, in the collieries the horses could not understand the language of their drivers. The reading of light literature was exchanged for Bible reading, and shops were cleared of their stocks of Bibles and Testaments. Prayer meetings were held in collieries underground, in trains and all kinds of places. Jesse Penn-Lewis *The Awakening in Wales*

As we reflect on what the Lord did in the past and compare these times with the present state of our twenty-first-century Church, it becomes clear that we need a similar work of God today. Unlike previous times, today's Church has been on the back foot for several generations, defending itself from the onslaughts of Secularist Religion. In the next chapter, we will see that the Lord is ready and willing to again step down into human affairs. He will do this when His people recognize their need, humble themselves before Him and call on His help. He has done this before, and He will do it again.

Six

RE-DIGGING THE ANCIENT WELLS

> Our country is in great need of a spiritual awakening... I've gone from city to city and I have wept as I have seen how far people have moved from God. Billy Graham, *The Cross*

Can it happen again?

The cultural revolution of the past 50 years has resulted in secularism becoming the dominant influence in Western civilization. It has enshrined itself in our education systems, entertainment industries, news sources, and the halls of political power. Here in Australia, both sides of the political spectrum seek media support and so kowtow before secularism's high priests. The incessant bleating of secularists proclaims that their way is the only way, and nothing must stand in the way of their agenda. Voters view the major political parties as unrepresentative and increasingly supporting rich and powerful interests.

Consequently, people feel ignored, powerless, and unable to withstand the erosion of their liberties, especially freedom of religion and freedom of conscience. The secularist propaganda produces a feeling nothing can stop this social juggernaut. This may be true from a human perspective, but it overlooks the reality that God is not dead. He is fully capable of reversing the tide of godlessness—He stepped into history previously when His people were in great need, and He can do it again now.

> When may a revival be expected? When the wickedness of the wicked grieves and distresses the Christian. Billy Sunday (1862-1935)

> The teaching of the Bible and the evidence from church history indicate that the age of miracles has not passed.

God can and will step down and turn the tide of godlessness when His people call on Him for help and do what is necessary to prepare the way for Him to do His work. Both local revival and a widespread awakening are possible and within the prayer possibilities of today's church. Added to the clear teaching of God's Word, we can be encouraged by what the Lord has done in the past. The idea we can do nothing to change the present trajectory is a lie from the kingdom of darkness.

For those concerned that seeking revival is not scriptural or undermining God's sovereignty, we must refer to God's Word as our authority. Interestingly, a Calvinist wrote the tract that has arguably been most influential in motivating people to pray for revival through the years. He urged his people to claim God's promises to bless them by calling on Him in Prayer. Jonathan Edwards (1703-1758), who wrote 'An Humble Attempt,' pointed to God's great promises in the Old Testament. They motivated God's people to seek His face for revival in their day:

> 'Arise, shine; For your light has come! And the glory of the LORD is risen upon you. For behold, the darkness shall cover the earth, and deep darkness the people; But the LORD will arise over you, And His glory will be seen upon you. The Gentiles shall come to your light, And kings to the brightness of your rising' (Isaiah 60:1-3).

2 Chronicles 7:14 is another scripture universally accepted as a motivator for revival. It has been quoted repeatedly by those who sought God for a new work of God in their day. At the dedication of the Temple that he had built, King Solomon asked the Lord if His people could come before Him in times of need and seek His help. God's response was immediate and unconditional. Yes!

> If My people who are called by My name will humble themselves, and pray and seek My face, and turn from their wicked ways, then I will hear from heaven and will forgive their sin and heal their land. (2 Chronicles 7:14)

This is an Old Testament passage, and some aspects of God's reply to Solomon apply only to the Jewish nation. For example, God gave them their land as a part of His covenant, but today there is no such thing as a Christian country. Having said that, when Jesus cleansed the Temple of the merchandisers, He made it clear that God intended the Temple as a house of prayer. When Jesus taught His disciples to pray, He explained that we serve a God who answers His people's prayers because of our unique relationship with the Father. He has done so throughout the many centuries, and it is for this reason prayer has become the recognized precursor of revival.

Remembering the ancient wells

Throughout the Bible, the Lord instructs His people to remember His past dealings with them. His motive was to develop faith in their hearts, preparing them for His future mighty works. The devil wants us to believe that there is no hope, that we are powerless against today's bleak secularism that saturates the marketplace of ideas. However, we should be encouraged. The Lord has visited His people with revival before, and He can do so again.

All the major Christian denominations were either born out of awakenings or have experienced a revival at some time in their history. This means that our mainstream churches have a rich spiritual heritage they can draw on today. This doesn't mean that we can turn back the clock and revisit those former times, but it does mean that we can rediscover spiritual principles and truths that can be leveraged and applied by today's church. By exploring the depths of God's timeless Word, we can rediscover those truths and dynamics that produced revival and awakenings in previous generations.

> I am convinced that the Lord wants to bring new life to old denominations and movements, which can happen when they rediscover how to access God's rich resources and blessings from the ancient wells.

Previous generations were similarly powerless against the godlessness of their times. Still, they learned how to leverage their weakness and tap into the spiritual resources that are the birthright of all believers. This present generation needs to find again and unblock the ancient wells of living water.

In His conversation with a Samaritan woman, Jesus used a communal well as a metaphor for the living water that He alone offers. Every human being thirsts for His living water, but many ignore the genuine article in their frantic search for a godless substitute.

> Jesus answered and said to her, "If you knew the gift of God, and who it is who says to you, 'Give Me a drink,' you would have asked Him, and He would have given you living water."
> John 4:10

Jacob's Well is a powerful symbol of the source of spiritual life in Jesus Christ. Just as physical water is necessary to sustain life in the Middle East's arid desert areas, we also need the living water of the Holy Spirit to maintain our spiritual life today.

Jacob's father, Isaac, made his living as a shepherd. To keep his livestock alive, he couldn't afford to take risks. So instead of prospecting unexplored territory during an intense drought, he turned to his father Abraham's ancient wells. However, the wells had been deliberately filled with debris by the Philistines, his traditional enemies. They had also changed the names of the wells to confuse their rightful owners. Nevertheless, these wells were a part of Isaac's rich heritage from his father, and it was these wells that he re-dug to access the life-giving water.

> And Isaac dug again the wells of water which they had dug in the days of Abraham his father, for the Philistines had stopped them up after the death of Abraham. He called them by the names which his father had called them. Also, Isaac's servants dug in the valley, and found a well of running water there. Genesis 26:18-19

Jesus' message is just as relevant today as it was back at Jacob's well. Materialism will never satisfy man's spiritual thirst in the long term. His new car provides a short-term buzz but only leaves him wanting next year's model. Beyond this material world are limitless supplies of heavenly grace and blessing in Jesus Christ. Our humanity is made complete in Him alone—our great spiritual thirst quencher!

> In the Bible, wells sometimes symbolize blessings from the hand of the Lord. The Church keeps looking for something new when all we need is to dig again the old wells of spiritual life that God's people have depended on from the beginning—the Word of God, prayer, worship, faith, the power of Spirit, sacrifice, and service—wells that we've allowed the enemy to fill up. Whenever there's been a revival of spiritual power in the history of the church, it's been because somebody has dug again the old wells so that God's life-giving Spirit can be free to work.[77] Warren Wiersbe

In John's Gospel, Jesus took the imagery even further, stating that believers could drink from His well and living water would overflow those who trust in Him. The same outpouring of God's rivers of living water is essential for changing our 21st-century world. Crowds witnessed the overflow when He poured out His Holy Spirit on the Day of Pentecost. The same Spirit gushed through the Church's awakenings and revivals through the centuries. When God steps into human history, believers from all theological backgrounds experience the resources that God had always intended to bestow upon His Church.

> On the last day, that great day of the feast, Jesus stood and cried out, saying, "If anyone thirsts, let him come to me and drink. "He who believes in me, as the Scripture has said, out of his heart will flow rivers of living water." But this He spoke concerning the Spirit, whom those believing in Him would receive; for the Holy Spirit was not yet given, because Jesus was not yet glorified. John 7:37-39

Today's Church must rediscover the spiritual life experienced by past generations. Living water is still available today, but first, the wells must be rediscovered and re-dug. Once the wells are open, today's Church can drink and renew its intended vitality. Only then can the living water that Jesus offers overflow God's people and saturate the lost world. Many lost souls accepted the overflow during past awakenings and revivals—this is our dire need today.

> Our Lord says to the Apostle, 'Tarry in Jerusalem,' as if to say: I have taught you how, I have instructed you; you have the knowledge; but you cannot do this, you cannot be witnesses unto me until you have been baptized with the Holy Spirit. So, wait until… Then… That is what you find throughout the running centuries.[78] Martyn Lloyd-Jones

---

Evil confederacies have attacked God's people in the ancient past, but He always responded when they humbled themselves and prayed.

The same pattern has occurred in the more recent awakenings. When His people recognize their abject poverty of spirit and seek His help, He has stepped down and done a 'new thing.' As a result, massive revivals are already sweeping through non-Western countries where believers have embraced the truth of God's word and cried out to Him.

However, when His people are self-satisfied and content to build the Kingdom of God in their own strength, He still loves them but will stand back and wait until they realize just how much they need His help.

Today, as the Church remembers its spiritual inheritance and learns to unblock the ancient wells, it will once more enter a new era of victory and fruitfulness. We need to be like Elisha, who learned from Elijah, the godly prophet of the previous generation. The spiritual needs of people all around us are immense, and the Gospel has lost none of its power to save. Therefore, the Church must once more learn how to access the spiritual resources that are their God-given birthright.

A template for revival and awakening

As we reflect on God's response to previous generations of believers that urgently sought Him, a pattern emerges. Because of this, the prayer movement that ignited the Second Great Awakening in Britain could be considered a template for awakening and reviving His people. Following a call for united prayer in the English Midlands, the Second Great Awakening in Great Britain ignited. Its influence crossed the Atlantic, inspiring people in the United States to seek the Lord for revival. The Third Great Awakening, and other revivals of the 19th and 20th centuries, have followed this same pattern.

Awakening generally describes the impact of the Lord stepping down to help His people in time of need. Although these awakenings are God's sovereign work and are something man can't produce, every revival in history began with prayer: sustained, intentional, united prayer. The Prayer Call of 1784 is an inspiring example.

> Every revival in history began in prayer:
> Sustained, intentional, united prayer.

In 2012, while visiting the U.K., my wife and I had the privilege to attend a worship service at the Fuller Baptist Church in Kettering, Northamptonshire. The Gospel mightily impacted this small market town in the late 18th and early 19th centuries, and this very church building hosted the formation of the Baptist Missionary Society (BMS) in 1792. After the service, I learned some intriguing facts as we toured the church building. Built during a time of revival, the seating capacity of the building was 1500 people. Therefore, it was necessary to hold multiple meetings each week to cater to demand. Not only that, soon after this building opened, another Baptist church building of similar size opened in another part of town. There was also a thriving Anglican Church and others of different denominations. In those early days, Kettering's population was 3,000, so close to 100% must have been involved in the mighty move of God.

Further research indicated that before he went to India as a missionary, William Carey conducted youth meetings in the Fuller Church with 1000 people in attendance. When you do the arithmetic, you cannot help wondering that something unusual must have taken place to pack churches in an age of growing skepticism and social decline. So, what happened? The simple answer is that this region became the epicenter of the Second Great Awakening that swept both Great Britain and America. And it all started with prayer.

The revival origins could be traced to three local ministers, members of the local Baptist Association, inspired by a tract on prayer by Jonathan Edwards in New England. Edwards' book A Humble Attempt called for widespread prayer, calling on the Lord to fulfill His purposes on earth and pour out the blessings promised in His word. This book's message gripped the hearts of these local ministers, John Ryland, Andrew Fuller, and John Sutcliff, and motivated them to pray, seeking God for revival. In 1784, Andrew Fuller preached a sermon, and in true Baptist fashion, John Sutcliff moved a motion to challenge the members of their Association to set time aside once a month for prayer. This Prayer Call of 1784, as it became known, began with these words:

> Upon a motion being made to the ministers and messengers of the associate Baptist churches assembled at Nottingham, respecting meetings for prayer, to bewail the low estate of religion, and earnestly implore a revival of our churches, and of the general cause of our Redeemer, and for that end **to wrestle with God for the effusion of his Holy Spirit**, which alone can produce the blessed effect.[79] [Emphasis added]

In their formal 18th century English, they were concerned that their society was going down the tubes and that their churches could not turn the tide. They needed God's help! Their earnest prayer implored God to revive the church, as He had done 50 years previously in the First Great

Awakening. In case the people didn't get it the first time, Sutcliff went on to make his purpose abundantly clear:

> The grand object of prayer is to be that the Holy Spirit may be poured down on our ministers and churches, that sinners may be converted, the saints edified, the interest of religion revived, and the name of God glorified. Prayer Call of 1784

Over the next few years, as churches met for prayer, God moved in a new way. Within the declining Baptist Churches, the tide started to turn. Membership grew, as did the number of churches. By 1798 there were 361 Baptist churches, more than double 40 years before. By 1812, the number had risen to 532' [80]. By the time C.H. Spurgeon (1834-1892) had begun his ministry, the number of Baptist churches in England had grown to 1400.

The call to prayer was crucial but not the only factor. Andrew Fuller came to know Jesus personally, then broke with the Calvinist tradition of those days and began proclaiming the Gospel to unbelievers inside and outside the church. He reasoned that if Jesus did this, he was on safe ground theologically. In so doing, he discovered large numbers of people were thirsting for spiritual truth.

As a result, people began turning to God in droves. William Carey (1761-1834), a local shoemaker turned pastor and a member of Sutcliff's church caught the vision for world evangelism. Carey took a one-way trip to Serampore in India at significant personal cost. Today, Carey is renowned as the Father of Modern Missions and inspired other denominations to take the Gospel to nations that had never heard it.

Today, there are an estimated 29 million Christians in India,[81] and the whole missionary enterprise arose from a prayer movement. When missionaries set forth, they "expected great things from God and attempted great things for God." For example, the Rev John Saunders arrived in Sydney, Australia, in 1832: 'Encouraged and commissioned, though not supported, by the Baptist Missionary Society.[82] This historic move was the beginning of the Baptist Church in Australia.

News of the prayer movement that had spread all over Britain reached America, and they too began to seek God for another Awakening. Like their brothers and sisters in England, they started concerts of prayer, and the Lord soon began to move in great power.

The situation in America followed the familiar pattern as their Second Great Awakening burst forth. American society was in severe decline, with their churches dying. Not many people realize it, but there was severe moral deterioration in the wake of the American Revolution (1775-1783). According to J. Edwin Orr, drunkenness became epidemic; out of a population of five million, 300,000 were hopeless drunkards. Profanity was of the most shocking kind. For the first time in the history of the American settlement, women were afraid to go out at night for fear of assault. Bank robberies were a daily occurrence.[83] Then the passion for prayer brought a fresh move of God.

> In New England, there was a man of prayer named Isaac Backus, a Baptist pastor, who in 1794, when conditions were at their worst, addressed an urgent plea for prayer for revival to pastors of every Christian denomination in the United States. Churches knew that their backs were to the wall. All the churches adopted the plan until America, like Britain was interlaced with a network of prayer meetings, which set aside the first Monday of each month to pray. It was not long before revival came. J. Edwin Orr [84]

The Second Great Awakening impacted millions of people in the USA. This awakening had a 'greater impact on secular society than any other in American history through its vast social concern.' In Kentucky thousands attended Camp Meetings. It is not an exaggeration to say that this awakening, more than anything else, shaped American society in its formative years.

> During the first three decades of the 1800s, Lewis Tappan and many other influential Christian laypeople organized thousands of societies that touched every phase of American life. Slavery, temperance, vice, world peace, women's rights, Sabbath observance, prison reform, profanity, education— all these and more had specific societies devoted to their betterment. Christianity Today [87]

This Second Great Awakening in America was so incendiary that it had a profound effect on overseas visitors like French academic and political scientist Alexis de Tocqueville (1805-1859). De Tocqueville visited America in 1831-1832 and was impressed by what he saw in this new Republic. In his best-selling and highly influential book Democracy in America, de Tocqueville wrote:

> I sought for the greatness and genius of America in her commodious harbors and her ample rivers—and it was not there . . . in her fertile fields and boundless forests and it was not there . . . in her rich mines and her vast world commerce—and it was not there . . . in her democratic Congress and her matchless Constitution—and it was not there. Not until I went into the churches of America and heard her pulpits aflame with righteousness did I understand the secret of her genius and power. America is great because she is good, and if America ever ceases to be good, she will cease to be great. Alexis de Tocqueville

When the revival fires that had burned throughout the early decades of the 19th century began to die down, another awakening broke out and became known as the Third Great Awakening. It, too, was birthed in prayer. The Lord led Jeremiah Lanphier to establish a prayer meeting in Fulton St, Lower Manhattan in New York City in 1857. Only a handful of people attended until a few weeks later, when the stock market crashed on October 10, everything changed.

As New York's population faced the bottom falling out of their world, hitting the wall produced an avalanche of prayer. Some 10,000 people gathered for prayer daily in New York City alone.[88] Newspapers like the New York Herald and the New York Tribune picked up the story, and interest in this prayer movement spread worldwide. The effects of this revival went around the world to places like Korea and Northern Ireland in 1859. This third awakening also birthed the evangelistic ministry of DL Moody in Chicago and the Holiness Movement.

It is impossible to escape the importance of united prayer in spiritual awakenings. Prayer launched the last national revival in Great Britain—the Awakening in Wales (1904-1905). Wales had experienced several awakenings previously, impacted by the First, Second, and Third Great Awakenings. However, towards the end of the 19th century, there was growing recognition of the need for another move of God. One of the most helpful accounts I have read on the Welsh Revival is *The Awakening in Wales* by Jesse Penn-Lewis. This short book traces the effects of the revival and the various springs and streams associated with a mighty river of blessing.

Especially interesting is that events in Melbourne, Australia motivated people in Wales to pray for their revival. The Welsh heard about the prayer circles that preceded evangelist R.A. Torrey's outreach meetings in Melbourne, and they were encouraged to pray for revival. The results are apparent.

> At Keswick in 1902—the first I had ever attended— 'Prayer Circles' were announced for a 'Worldwide Revival.' Then I went to the Lord and cried, 'Lord, why must they pray for what Thou hast already promised?' Then He said, 'This Revival is an accomplished fact in My Kingdom,' and I said, 'Why does it not come, Lord, without these Prayer Circles? He replied, 'I am ready, but My children are not. Before it comes, they must preach the word of the Cross—the message of Calvary. Jesse Penn-Lewis *The Awakening in Wales* [89]

R.A. Torrey, a colleague and associate of D.L. Moody, had been invited to conduct a series of meetings in Melbourne in 1902—just one year after the Australian Federation, the nation's birth, in 1901. Before this evangelistic campaign, thousands of people met for prayer in homes right across the city. The impact was such that when Melbourne's population was 500,000, an estimated 250,000 attended meetings at the Royal Exhibition Building. And here is the interesting part. Although many came to know the Lord, and rich blessings arose from these meetings, it didn't produce a regional, let alone a national revival. (I believe the Lord has reserved that blessing for the 21st century!) However, in Wales, when people at a Keswick Conference heard about the circles of prayer in Melbourne, they too decided they would intensify their prayer effort. So, once again, history reveals that the people of Wales enjoyed their revival, solidly founded on prayer.

> Prayer preceded the first Pentecost, and PRAYER must precede the wider outpouring of the Spirit in the last days, therefore the true members of Christ all over the world must be drawn by the Spirit within them into one accord in asking God to pour forth His Spirit according to His word. The extent of the one will govern the extent of the other, for prayer prepares the channels for the Holy Spirit to fill, and flow out through into the world. Jesse Penn Lewis *The Awakening in Wales*

Seven

CALLING ON THE NAME OF THE LORD

> To clasp the hands in prayer is the beginning of an uprising against the disorder of the world. Karl Barth. (1886-1968) [90]

There is a reason that every revival and awakening in history began in prayer. When people find themselves in situations without human solutions, they turn to prayer, calling on the Lord for His help. Furthermore, spiritual decline usually causes desperate circumstances that people cannot address independently. Whether it is the children of Israel suffering Egyptian slavery or the bondage of exile in Babylon, the Bible records that people usually only get serious with God when they hit the wall and have no alternative. The West's departure from faith in God in the past 50 years ought to have driven every Christian to their knees long ago.

The Biblical record

Adam and Eve's rebellion against God produced sin, the fatal flaw that ultimately infected the whole human race. In the case of Adam and Eve, the result of their rebellion was that their son Cain murdered his brother Abel. After this horrific tragedy, Adam and Eve conceived another son named Seth, and when he too became a father and Adam and Eve became grandparents, they all began to pray. They began to call on the name of the Lord for his help and support. Their whole family had experienced the pain and heartache resulting from their family dysfunction, so when Enosh was born, they knew they needed God's help.

> And as for Seth, to him also a son was born; and he named him Enosh. **Then men began to call on the name of the Lord.**
> Genesis 4:26 [Emphasis added]

Parenting is never easy and is particularly challenging for first-time parents who have never done it before. Adam and Eve had no positive role models, and Seth wanted to avoid his parents' parenting pitfalls. Parents have no way of knowing if they are on track apart from clear guidelines or a reliable role model. If a child loses its way in adolescence, it is often too late for the parents to correct their parenting plan. When Seth became a father for the first time, he realized he needed to avoid his parent's mistakes to evade the past heartache and pain. And so, parents and grandparents alike recognized their need for God's help, and it was then that they (collectively) began to call on the name of the Lord.

God had promised these parents and grandparents a Savior [91] who would redeem them from Satan's nefarious rebellion against the King of Heaven. However, when Abel, a godly man, was murdered, their hopes of a quick resolution were dashed.

> If their family was to survive and prosper, they needed God's help. In recognition of their complete failure as parents and grandparents, and out of concern for the next generation, they acknowledged their dire need. They started crying out to the Lord for help

There is no more compelling reason to cry out to God for His help than for the welfare of our descendants. The present generation has rejected our traditional foundations and sought to remove the influence of Christianity from Western Civilization. Consequently, they walk through life without a moral compass. Their only guide is the confused wisdom of man, but in their post-truth society, they face conflicting opinions, not knowing who or what to trust. Without the traditional wisdom of their Christian heritage, they navigate the waters of their post-truth world through a maelstrom of confusion. For several generations, wise voices warned the West of the consequences of rejecting the Gospel. Still, it is only now that we face the devastating reality of a society with no foundation, identity, or direction.

> I consider that the chief dangers which confront the coming century will be religion without the Holy Ghost; Christianity without Christ; forgiveness without repentance; salvation without regeneration; politics without God; and Heaven without Hell. Salvation Army General William Booth (1829-1912)

We are emerging from the COVID pandemic into a world that we are told faces climate change extinction. Consequently, the millennial generation is the first in 2000 years to face a future without certainty. They have no realistic hope that their future will be brighter than their parent's. History proves that all man's attempts to save himself apart from God have failed, and the millennial generation will carry the burden of a similar failure. Likewise, all secularists' attempts at achieving a utopian society apart from God have come to nothing. Now the millennial generation finds themselves alone without God and hope[92] in an increasingly chaotic and hostile world.

The believer's spiritual battle

Only when the Church recognizes that it faces a spiritual battle of cosmic proportions will it accept that mere human resolve is woefully inadequate. No political, social, or economic resolution can turn the tide of the encroaching gloom and confusion. When the Church faces the stark truth of society's moral bankruptcy and its contributing negligence, it can legitimately repent and petition the Lord for His help. The tide can only turn when the Church once more makes it a priority to call on the name of the Lord. Then He will unleash His almighty power. Then, at last, everything will change!

Instead of fighting a cultural battle so stacked against it that it can never win, the Church will step up to fight the spiritual battle that it cannot lose.

The Church must experience the reality of the ancient struggle between light against darkness, and good against evil. Its need is for spiritual armor and weaponry that it may be 'strong in the Lord and the power of His might.'[93]

The First Century Church understood that its God-given mission was to turn people from darkness to The Light. They knew the pagan world was trapped in a massive delusion, and their mission was 'to open their eyes, to turn them from darkness to light, and from the power of Satan to God' (Acts 26:18). To accomplish this mission, the Church employed two God-given spiritual resources for the light to shine; the word of God and prayer. The apostle Paul explained to the Ephesian Church that all believers are engaged in a supernatural fight of light against darkness. However, the Lord had not only graciously provided spiritual armor for their defense[94] and protection, but also formidable weaponry against the pagan darkness and the accompanying confusion. These, together with other weapons such as the Name of Jesus and the blood of the Cross, not only protected against the enemy's attacks but also were powerful to bring down the entrenched spiritual strongholds of paganism.[95]

> There are two kinds of means requisite to promote a revival: the one to influence man, the other to influence God. The truth is used to influence men, and prayer to influence God. [96] Charles G. Finney

Overcoming feelings of disempowerment

One of the signs of our times is the sense of disempowerment in Western society. There is a growing sense that the opinions of the individual citizens no longer matter, that no one is listening. Instead of representing the aspirations of their constituents, the crucial decisions are made by political elites who push their private agenda.

While the West prides itself on its democratic foundations, there is a sense that the present political machinery no longer meets peoples' expectations. Increasingly, those who shout loudest get heard, those who push hardest get their way, and those with the most dollars influence policy direction. Having abandoned its Christian birthright, the West is reverting to the law of the jungle. Paganism is about the survival of the fittest and the belief that might-makes-right. Consequently, the weaker, less vocal—that is, most people, feel their voices aren't heard. As a result, only the rich, powerful, and well-connected get to shape our direction. This sense of being ignored has led to disempowerment, expressing itself in random, haphazard, and volatile political direction. Those on the left are moving further left, while the right is moving further right.

These same feelings of disempowerment have now permeated the Church. Most believers appear unable to counter the encroaching darkness. In previous generations, believers would cry out to God in times of crisis, whereas today, secular society doubts whether God exists or, if He does, is willing to help. Anecdotally, only a shrinking minority rises above the confusion to believe that God can and will respond to revival prayer.

Instead of calling on the Lord for revival, there appear to be three alternative responses to the current militant secularism. The first and most common is that the Church believes it only needs to tweak its modus operandi to reach unbelievers and evangelize the world. Sadly, however, the Church has been struggling for decades to be 'relevant' while it continues to slide backward. Another fallacious response is that awakenings are a sovereign work of God, so any attempt to seek revival is a challenge to His authority. However, this denies the teaching of scripture that the Lord answers the prayers of His people. Man can't do God's part, and He won't do man's part, which means calling on Him for His help. Finally, another deep-seated hindrance to revival is that many Christians are convinced it is too late; the appearance of the Antichrist is imminent, so we must hang on till Jesus returns to rescue His Church. This view ignores the promises of God that He will pour out His Spirit in the last days (Acts 2:18-20).

The prophecy of Joel that Peter quoted in his Pentecostal sermon spoke of cosmic upheavals with 'wonders in heaven above and signs in the earth beneath' (see also Matthew 24:29, Mark 13:24, Revelation 6:12). The sun turned into darkness and the moon into blood haven't happened yet, making Joel's prophecy incomplete. Whatever your view of the timeline of Jesus' return, scripture teaches that His coming will be preceded by a mighty outpouring of the Holy Spirit: 'I will pour out My Spirit in those days.. before the coming of the great and awesome day of the Lord' (Acts 2:18, 2:20).

Despite attempts to downplay the existential threat facing the Church, a growing number of believers recognize the desperate need for the Lord to do something new. Sadly, however, many who yearn for revival suffer disempowerment because they have no idea where to start. Miracles of grace occur when God's people recognize their need and humbly call to Him. That is, when they get real and begin to do business with God. Someone asked the English evangelist Gypsy Smith (1860-1947) how to have a revival; "Go home, lock yourself in a closet. Kneel in the middle of the floor and draw a chalk circle around yourself. Ask God to send revival inside that chalk circle. When God answers your prayers, then revival will come!"

My advice to those who yearn for revival is to call on the Lord for His help. If your heart is crying out for Him to move in a new way and no one else appears to be listening, ask the Lord to bring you to another person of like mind. Then, once you have a prayer partner, you can pray together for a third member and initiate a prayer triplet. Pray for the Lord to bless your church leaders, and fellow believers in your local Church. Intercede for your community. Ask Him to step down and move in the same way He has done so many times in the past.

Great power is unleashed when a believer prays, but this effect is multiplied when believers pray together

---

Jesus taught His disciples, 'if two of you agree on earth concerning anything that they ask, it will be done for them by My Father in heaven. For where two or three are gathered in My name, I am there in the midst of them (Matthew 18:19-20). There is a spiritual principle. When two or three people meet in Jesus' name, He has promised to honor their faith by being in their midst. Even if only two believers agree on anything in prayer, Jesus has promised that He will grant their request. Here is the Biblical answer to the prevalent feelings of disempowerment that assault us. Our political masters may not care enough to listen to the cries of our hearts, but our Father in heaven will.

Many examples in both scripture and history illustrate the power and effectiveness of small group prayer, even if there are only two or three. Moses, for example, had Aaron and Hur strengthen his hands as he upheld the rod of God. So too, David had his three mighty men who gave support and allegiance to his cause. As well as the twelve disciples, Jesus Himself had an inner group of Peter, James, and John who were with Him in an extraordinarily close relationship. So too, when the Lord ignites revival, it often begins with just the twos and threes of praying people.

The story of the 1859 Ulster Revival in Ireland began with the conversion of a young man named James McQuilkin. He, in turn, shared the Gospel with some friends. Then, McQuilkin and three of his friends met in a schoolhouse to pray for revival. Soon others joined them, and the Ulster Revival burst into flame. The Lord heard the cries of this small group of believers who called on Him in heartfelt prayer.

The example of Jehoshaphat

While the New Testament believer's spiritual battle is truth versus lies and delusion, the Old Testament records many physical battles where the Children of Israel defended themselves from their enemies. These battles also carried a spiritual dimension, where prayer decided their outcome.

The story of Jehoshaphat is one of many, many accounts from the word of God that illustrates the victory of God's people in physical and spiritual warfare. When an implacable foe confronted God's people, they turned to the Lord in prayer and sought His assistance. When Jehoshaphat heard that a confederacy of traditional enemies was preparing to attack, he instructed his people to pray and seek the Lord. He recognized the seriousness of the situation and the existential threat they faced. Humanly speaking, they were outgunned and outnumbered, so calling on the Lord in fasting and prayer was their only option.

> And Jehoshaphat feared, and set himself to seek the LORD, and proclaimed a fast throughout all Judah. 2 Chronicles 20:3

The background to this drama is that Jehoshaphat was a godly king who followed the Lord, but his circumstances changed through no fault of his own. It is important to note that the threats from Israel's traditional enemies were not because of anything they had done but simply because they were the people of God. Their enemies were jealous of the way God had blessed them and wanted to bring them down. However, by waging war against God's people, they were also against the Lord Himself. Jehoshaphat knew that he could rely on the Lord to step down and help them when they called on Him for help. The two things that motivated Jehoshaphat to pray were first: they were outgunned and outnumbered, and secondly that they had no idea what to do in this impossible situation. Jehoshaphat's prayer was simply a reliance that God would help when asked appropriately.

> O our God, will You not judge them? For we have no power against this great multitude that is coming against us; nor do we know what to do, but our eyes are upon You. 2 Chronicles 20:12

Jehoshaphat was humble enough to know there was no political solution to his nation's problem; God was their only hope. So, they called on Him in their time of grave peril, and He responded; He stepped down into human history to help. When they cried out in prayer, the Lord spoke to them directly and confirmed His promise to act on their behalf, telling them not to be afraid; His promises were good enough. Their faith was not in vain despite the human impossibility of their situation. The enemy was only attacking them because they were God's covenant people, and accordingly, He would step in to help.

> And he said, "Listen, all you of Judah and you inhabitants of Jerusalem, and you, King Jehoshaphat! Thus says the LORD to you: **'Do not be afraid nor dismayed because of this great multitude, for the battle is not yours, but God's.** 2 Chronicles 20:15 [Emphasis added]

In any physical conflict, the enemy will always attempt to gain an advantage by psychological means. Truth is one of the first casualties of war, and propaganda can be as destructive as arrows or bullets. In Jehoshaphat's day, his army was in danger of losing hope and giving up because the enemies of God's people attempted to disseminate lies, falsehood, and disinformation. The Trojan horse subterfuge was not the only time armies used deception in battle. However, the Lord reminded His people of His promise to answer their prayers and help them. In this incident, the Lord told them they wouldn't even need to fight. The battle was the Lord's, and He would take care of everything.

> You will not need to fight in this battle. Position yourselves, stand still and see the salvation of the LORD, who is with you, O Judah and Jerusalem!' Do not fear or be dismayed; tomorrow go out against them, for the LORD is with you. 2 Chronicles 20:17

Our spiritual enemy still sows fear, doubt, and confusion about God's willingness to help us. Many of today's sincere believers question whether God will hear their prayers and act on their behalf. This is evidenced by the lack of specific, intentional, focused prayer for revival. The Church has been cursing the darkness for too long instead of turning to the light. Consequently, God's people are confused and divided about revival and whether we can expect it again in our day.

Accordingly, we urgently need spiritual leaders who will, like Jehoshaphat, lead their people to pray and trust the Lord. We need to be reminded of the Lord's consistent care for his people when he said, 'do not fear or be dismayed. For the *LORD* is with you' (2 Chronicles 20:17).

As in the days of Jehoshaphat, the Lord's willingness to protect, bless, and revive His people is abundantly illustrated by past awakenings, when He stepped down in dark times to answer the prayers of His people.

No power in heaven and earth can prevent God from moving when He chooses to do so. Whenever His people humble themselves and call on Him, He will always manifest the fullness of His presence and power. "So says the High and Lofty One who inhabits eternity, whose name is Holy: I dwell in the high and holy place, with him who has a contrite and humble spirit, to revive the spirit of the humble, and to revive the heart of the contrite ones". Isaiah 57:15

The Holy Spirit still unfolds His sublime truth to soft, contrite hearts that willingly learn from Him. God's nature is such that He resists the proud and stubborn. Instead, He fills yielded hearts to overflowing with His presence and glory. Even though our God is Lord of all and sovereignly moves according to His plans and purposes, He always acts in response to His people's prayers.

> I discovered an astonishing truth: God is attracted to weakness.
> He can't resist those who humbly and honestly admit how

desperately they need him. Our weakness, in fact, makes room for his power. Jim Cymbala [97]

When God's people become weary of their puny, fleshly attempts to build their shabby imitations of what only God can create, awakenings are ignited. When they hit the wall with their inability to change their lives, let alone their family and society, they then begin calling on His name. Seeking the Lord in prayer, pleading for His help, brought Him into Jehoshaphat's battle with power. *Will You not revive us again, that Your people may rejoice in You?* Psalms 85:6

The lessons of history

History is full of examples of individuals, families, groups, and even nations calling on the Lord for His help in times of trouble. Jesus came to make peace between heaven and earth so that we can all call on Him and ask for His help.

Western nations like England and America have been recipients of God's love and protection many times in their past. When they called on Him, He was wonderfully faithful and answered prayers in profound ways. A good example was the planned invasion of England by Spain in 1588. The Spanish Armada was superior in numbers and firepower to the English fleet, but they were defeated resoundingly when the people called on Him for help.

Britain experienced another of God's mighty miracles during the second world war. King George VI, the current British Queen's father, called for a National Day of Prayer, seeking God's help in the country's hour of dire need. He launched this appeal on Sunday, May 26, 1940, when his country faced imminent invasion by Nazi Germany. In a stirring broadcast, he called the people of Britain and the British Empire to commit their plight to God. The King and his Cabinet attended Westminster Abbey, while millions of his subjects in all parts of the Commonwealth and Empire immediately flocked to churches to unite in prayer. The whole nation was praying that Sunday, and the scenes outside Westminster Abbey were remarkable. Photographs show long queues of people who could not even get into the Abbey; it was so crowded! So much so that the following morning the Daily Sketch exclaimed, *'Nothing like it has ever happened before.'* [98]

The King and his military advisors understood their situation was grave and that attack was inevitable. The Germans were supremely confident of victory. The leaders of the United States believed the Germans would prevail, so they suspended the provision of supplies in the face of Britain's inevitable collapse. The British had no defense against the Nazi juggernaut. The Nazi Blitzkrieg had defeated the French, Belgian, and Dutch armies, so the way was open for their final assault on the defeated British army, sitting defenseless, awaiting destruction on the Dunkirk beaches. There was nothing to prevent the German invasion of England. With no other option, the King called on the entire nation to pray to God for His help.

A bizarre chain of events followed the National Day of Prayer. There was no human explanation for why the Nazi invasion of Britain failed. Militarily speaking, there was absolutely nothing on earth to stop them. The Germans had implemented their invasion plans flawlessly, and the British army was defenseless against the might of Nazi Germany. Of the 335,000 soldiers trapped on the beaches around Dunkirk, Britain hastily formed plans to attempt to rescue at least 20,000 to 30,000 men using small boats across the English Channel. However, by a series of miraculous events, the entire force of 335,000 Allied soldiers was rescued and ferried safely across the Channel to England!

In a speech in the House of Commons on June 4, Prime Minister Churchill called the extraordinary withdrawal 'a miracle of deliverance.'[99] God had indeed responded to the united prayers of millions of people, instigating miracles that contributed to the successful rescue of so many men.

- First, for some inexplicable reason, Hitler overruled his generals and ordered their armored divisions to halt their advance on Dunkirk. Had they proceeded, the British forces would have been destroyed.
- Secondly, a fierce storm grounded the German Luftwaffe squadrons, enabling the British troops to retreat to the beaches.
- Third, despite the Flanders storm that grounded the German air force, an unusual calm settled over the English Channel during the crucial days that followed. The Channel waters became as still as a millpond. A vast armada of small boats, big ships, warships, and privately-owned motor cruisers from British rivers and estuaries, in fact almost anything that floated, plied back and forth to rescue the men.

So, after calling on the Lord's help, the whole British army was evacuated despite being cut off and surrounded. This astonishing event gave fresh cause for hope, and the British Prime Minister, Winston Churchill, went on to give his famous speech where he vowed: 'We shall fight on the beaches, we shall fight on the landing grounds, we shall fight in the fields and in the streets, we shall fight in the hills. We shall never surrender!'

And the miracles didn't stop there. After the British army's evacuation from Dunkirk, the Germans launched their aerial campaign against Britain, generally known as the Battle of Britain. Although outnumbered, the Royal Air Force held out. After inflicting heavy losses on British airfields, the Germans inexplicably began to bomb London and other cities. The suspension of attacks on British airfields allowed the RAF to regroup and withstand the invasion. Following this second sequence of miraculous events, the Germans shelved their invasion plans and instead moved against Russia, taking the pressure off Britain. It allowed them to regroup and fight back later. Despite the almost certainty of invasion, Great Britain fought on and ultimately experienced complete victory in World War II.

There are many more accounts of God's protection during World War II. Many people who didn't usually attend Church turned to God during the war and in the following decades. Isaac Watts wrote one of the traditional hymns popular during the war years (1674-1748). The hymn, Our God, our help in ages past, was sung aboard HMS Prince of Wales when Prime Minister Churchill met with American President Franklin Delano Roosevelt in 1941.[100] It was also sung at Winston Churchill's funeral service in 1965, the largest state funeral in history attended by representatives from 112 nations. This hymn is a song of praise of God for His faithfulness over many centuries. It confirms our confidence that we can still call on Him for His help today.

Our God, our help in ages past,

Our hope for years to come,
Our shelter from the stormy blast,
And our eternal home.
—Isaac Watts

It is tragic that with the renewed historical interest in World Wars I and II, the story of God's faithfulness has been almost totally airbrushed from the records. Most of the generations that experienced the two World Wars have already passed from the scene, so the current millennial generation does not have access to these testimonies of faith. This post-truth generation desperately needs to hear about the God who loves them and will help them when they call on Him in prayer.

Waking the sleeping giant

Another World War II 'coincidence' occurred when the American aircraft carriers were out at sea when the Japanese attacked Pearl Harbor. After that 'day of infamy,' Admiral Yamamoto, the enemy commander, realized they had failed to win the decisive victory they had planned, even though they had won the battle. The Japanese mission to destroy the American fleet was incomplete, and...

> Recognizing the consequences of this failure, Admiral Yamamoto reported, "I fear we have woken a sleeping giant and filled him with a great resolve" [101]

Until this brazen attack, the United States had refused to be involved because they felt it wasn't their war. They were also in denial about Japanese intentions, despite the reliable intelligence to the contrary.

> The attack on Pearl Harbor was the final wake-up call for the American people; the entire nation was outraged that Japan had launched the cowardly attack before they had formally declared war. Pretending to be friends, they actively planned to kill as many people as possible.

The words of the Japanese admiral proved prophetic because the United States recognized its peril, and aroused from denial, it leveraged its immense resources to help defeat the enemy. Of course, no sane entity wants to go to war, but neutrality in a global conflict was no longer an option. The sleeping giant indeed awoke.

Long before the Pearl Harbor attack, the Japanese and their Nazi allies planned their aggressive agenda. They had deceptively taken advantage of the American desire for peace during their war preparations. However, once they launched their attack, there was no doubt about their intentions—the American people developed steely resolve. Capitulation was not an option as the world's freedom was under threat.

Today's Church needs to awaken to the existential threats it faces from the spiritual powers of darkness. It must acknowledge it is involved in a spiritual battle and realize that it too is at war. When the Church finally awakens, it too will be like arousing a sleeping giant filled with a terrible resolve. Today's Church must arrive at a place where it appreciates that its passivity, inaction, and neutrality are no longer an option.

For decades, the struggle to remove Christian influence from society has been fought by an implacable spiritual foe that cannot be appeased or ignored. The ferocity and intensity of these attacks mean that believers must now either capitulate to the forces of secularism and political correctness or take a stand.

Only when the Church acknowledges it is engaged in a spiritual battle will it be motivated to seek the spiritual resources available as its birthright. Then everything will change.

> Finally, my brethren, be strong in the Lord and in the power of His might. Put on the whole armor of God, that you may be able to stand against the wiles of the devil. For we do not wrestle against flesh and blood, but against principalities, against powers, against the rulers of the darkness of this age, against spiritual hosts of wickedness in the heavenly places. Ephesians 6:10-12)

Eight

THE BIBLICAL PATTERN OF AWAKENINGS

> And the Lord, whom you seek, will suddenly come to His temple, Even the Messenger of the covenant, in whom you delight. Behold, He is coming," Says the LORD of hosts.
> Malachi 3:1

What is revival?

The term revival describes the new life that comes to an individual or church when brought into a closer, more intimate relationship with God.

> Revival produces a transformation in man's heart. He turns from selfishness to love, unbelief to faith, and control by his old sinful nature to being filled with the Holy Spirit. In short, revival is simply a turning from complacent carnal existence to the purity of the New Testament standard of radical faith and devotion to God.

Sometimes this revolution happens at conversion, as with the three thousand saved on the day of Pentecost. With others, it occurs through the sanctifying work of the Holy Spirit as a believer walks with the Lord and grows in faith. Thus, revival sometimes begins with a crisis and at other times through a steady growth in grace through which believers arrive at dedication and consecration to God.

One of the biggest hindrances to revival down through the ages has been unrealistic and unbiblical expectations. Jesus was rejected by the religious leaders of His day mainly because they expected somebody quite different from what God intended. They wanted a geopolitical leader or king, whereas Jesus came to establish His spiritual kingdom in the hearts of men. Therefore, we need a clear Biblical picture of how God ignites revival in human hearts. Of course, no two stories are alike. Still, as we examine how God brings revival to His people, a pattern emerges that will hopefully inspire us to seek His face for revival today.

Revival is not what people think!

When people think of revival and awakening, they generally envisage thousands of people flocking to hear the Gospel, with whole communities turning to God. As wonderful as these things are, we must understand that these are the fruit of the revival previously ignited in the hearts of perhaps only one or two people. It began with a fire of holy love kindled in the heart of a sincere believer, or perhaps with a small group of people who were seeking the Lord together. Of course, this happens differently in each believer. Nevertheless, it frequently follows a pattern that is often quite different from what people expect.

The experience of Dr. Joe Church (1899-1989) illustrated God's sovereign actions when he was a medical missionary serving in East Africa during the mid-twentieth century. Having experienced the East African Revival, he returned home to England to share his experiences at conferences and church meetings. In a conversation with his friend Roy Hession, Dr. Church explained the difference between genuine revival and the common perception. He said it is not about the top blowing off someone's life so much as the bottom falling out. It isn't about the achievements or success of some person or church that God rewards, but rather God's provision of grace for the disappointment and discouragement of His people. So often, the experience of failure produces the abject poverty of spirit that leads people to seek God and His help. And it generally begins when the individual has hit the wall in one way or another.

> The Christians of England, Roy, seem to have the strangest ideas of what revival really is, they think it is the roof blowing off, when it really is the bottom falling out! [102] Dr. Joe Church

Blessed are the poor in spirit

In Romans 1, the apostle Paul describes the downward spiral of a society that has rejected God. Reading this passage of scripture in a modern paraphrase is just like updating today's news. The Gospel reveals how Jesus has reversed this race to the bottom by lifting people to a new level of existence through His grace and love. In the beatitudes from the famous Sermon on the Mount, Jesus offers a step-by-step transformation of our human condition, elevating us to attain our fullest potential. The first and foundational of these keys to blessing, known as the beatitudes, is: "Blessed are the poor in spirit, for theirs is the kingdom of heaven" (Matthew 5:3).

> O the bliss of the man who has realized his whole utter helplessness, and who has put his whole trust in God, for thus alone he can render to God that perfect obedience which will make him a citizen of the kingdom of heaven. William Barclay *The Beatitudes*

Poverty of spirit occurs when believers open their spiritual eyes to see things as they are. As well as being able to see their sinfulness, they also become aware of God's holiness and moral perfection. Having been awakened, they retain no confidence in human effort, are emptied of self-reliance, and know their absolute insufficiency before God. The poor in spirit are blessed because they are dependent on the life and empowerment of the living God. Revival ignites when the individual is sufficiently humbled. Only then will a person see their actual condition before God. Then, and only then, will they turn to the Lord for His help, for He alone can satisfy the deepest longings of the human heart. When they do this, all the resources of heaven are at their disposal. God will save, transform, and lift them to fulfill His plans and purposes.

> Revival is having our spiritual eyes opened to see Jesus. William Ngenda. [103] Leader in the East African Revival

Most of those people the Lord mightily used in the Bible and the history of the Church lived lives characterized by a failure at some point in their spiritual journey. This failure revealed both their spiritual impotence and the mighty power, resources, and omnipotence of God.

> Moses began as a failure! That was the school from which he was qualified! Abraham began by being a failure! That was the school from which he qualified! Jacob was a hopeless failure! Elijah was a hopeless failure! Isaiah was a hopeless failure and a 'man of unclean lips', but it is in the school of destitution—the bitter school of self-discovery—that finally, you graduate into usefulness, when at last you discover the total bankruptcy of

> what you are apart from what God is! These men made this discovery and were blessed! Major Ian Thomas

Hitting the wall is an expression describing a crisis in life's journey. It happens when something unexpected comes up that doesn't merely slow our progress but stops it completely. When a vehicle hits the wall, everything stops. When someone hits the wall spiritually, they find themselves in a situation where only a miracle from heaven can help them. Human nature being what it is, it is when people hit the wall they begin to think about God in a new way and seek his help.

> God's time for revival is the very darkest hour, when everything seems hopeless. It is always the Lord's way to go to the very worst cases to manifest His glory. Andrew Gih

Many crucial spiritual life lessons are learned the hard way through personal experience. If the Exodus story is a biblical pattern of salvation and redemption, the story of the exile in Babylon and the later restoration is a biblical picture of revival. Revival is about the hearts of believers turning back to God. The various prophets, including Jeremiah, had warned God's people of the dangers of idolatry. Still, it wasn't until they went into captivity that they realized the implications of their choices. The exile from the land that God had given them was the supreme hitting-the-wall experience for God's people.

God had pleaded with them to humble themselves, reject their idolatry and turn their hearts to him, but with the exile, they hit the wall
---

However, the recognition of their failure made them candidates for grace and understand the love and grace of God in an even more profound way. After the exile, God's plan of restoration and revival kicked in.

Oswald Chambers (1874-1915) illustrates this revival process and how hitting the wall produces abject poverty of spirit. His famous devotional writings include My Utmost for His Highest, a blessing to believers over many generations. Their enduring appeal relates to their authenticity, resulting from the author's personal experience of personal revival. Chambers enjoyed a fruitful and effective ministry as an evangelist and author, later serving with distinction as a YMCA chaplain in World War I.

What is not generally known is that before he entered a walk of victory and fruitfulness, Oswald Chambers went through a time of spiritual conflict so severe that his biographer records he was on the verge of a complete breakdown. Chambers came to a place of defeat and crisis, believing that if what he was experiencing was all the Christian life offered, it was pointless to continue. This great man had hit the wall. While he had sought freedom from those personal sins that beset many young believers, he desperately wanted to be filled with the Holy Spirit, yet to no avail. Instead of the victory he sought, Chambers went through what many old-time preachers used to call the dark night of the soul. Instead of relief and release, his experience was one of sin and failure. Like the apostle Paul, the cry of Oswald Chambers' heart was, 'Wretched man that I am, who will deliver me?' (Romans 7:24). Chambers wrote:" The last three months of those years, things reached a climax, I was getting very desperate. I knew no one who had what I wanted; in fact, I did not know what I did want. But I knew that if what I had was all the Christianity there was, the thing was a fraud." [104]

However, right there, in brokenness and powerlessness, the Lord began to open his eyes in awful self-discovery. Then he awoke to a beautiful God-discovery that transformed his life. Isaiah 66:2 teaches us that God looks for people who are "humble and contrite in spirit and trembles at my word." In extreme poverty of spirit, Oswald Chambers began to cry out to God and made a total consecration of his life to his Lord. As described by his biographer, Oswald Chambers became a man abandoned to God. Mr. Chambers began to see Jesus in a new way, and God kindled a love for his Master in his heart.

Oswald's testimony is one of many anecdotes from the Bible and church history that illustrate the pattern of revival. Following seasons of failure and defeat, the Lord ignites flames of Holy love in the hearts of His servants. Filled to overflowing with the Love of God, victory over sin becomes just one of many by-products of a new relationship with our Savior.

> Glory be to God, the last aching abyss of the human heart is filled to overflowing with the love of God. Love is the beginning, love is the middle, and love is the end. After He comes in, all you see is 'Jesus only, Jesus ever.' When you know what God has done for you, the power and the tyranny of sin is gone and the radiant, the unspeakable emancipation of the indwelling Christ has come. Oswald Chambers [105]

The priority of prayer

Poverty of spirit creates a sense of dependency on the Lord that leads to the next step in the revival pattern: that is fervent, passionate, believing prayer. When we pray, we open the door to divine intervention as we invite God into our situation. Jesus stands at the door knocking (Revelation 3:20), but our active faith expressed in prayer opens the door to His working.

We see this principle illustrated in the life of Isaiah the prophet. In the year King Uzziah died, the prophet was in the Temple that the Lord had ordained to be a house of prayer. The death of Uzziah was a crushing disappointment because any hope of a political solution to the moral decline of the nation died with him. For Isaiah, this was about hitting the wall and beginning to do business with God in the Temple. In the house of prayer, he had an extraordinary vision of the Lord "sitting on a throne, high and lifted up, and the train of His robe filled the temple" (Isaiah 6:1). Believers in previous generations used to say that 'man's extremity is God's opportunity,' which was certainly the case with Isaiah. That is why every awakening in history followed fervent, desperate prayer: and when the prayer stops, so does the revival.

> There has never been a spiritual awakening in any country or locality that did not begin in united prayer. A.T. Pierson (1837-1911)

The Lord yearns for spiritual intimacy with His people, which is why Jesus taught His disciples to pray, 'Our Father in Heaven.' The desire to pray is the outworking of our heart-relationship with our heavenly Father. Heartfelt prayer is always the fruit of a renewed relationship with God as the believer cries out 'Abba, Father!' (Galatians 4:6). In the many accounts of revival and awakening throughout history, the Lord works in different ways to bring his people back to a close prayer relationship with Himself. Matthew Henry (1662-1714) said in his commentary on Zechariah 12:10, describing the pouring out of a Spirit of grace and supplication on his people; 'Note when God intends great mercy for his people the first thing he does is to set them a praying.'

God gave His people the temple in the Old Testament as a specific geographical location where they could call on Him day or night. This place was the only venue where sinful humanity could interface and talk with a Holy God. After His death and resurrection, Jesus represented the real temple, fulfilling a prophecy He spoke before He left them (John 2:19). The

Temple was God's idea, and it provided a way for flawed humanity to enter an intimate relationship with a Holy God.

Tragically, the exile denied God's people their right to access the house of prayer, and, while they were in Babylon, this separation birthed a longing to renew their face-to-face fellowship with God. However, prophets like Jeremiah and Isaiah saw beyond the immediate circumstances, and this separation was temporary. Isaiah prophesied that God would do a new thing and restore them to fellowship with Himself, and the time would come when He would listen to and answer their prayers once more.

> Then you shall call, and the LORD will answer; You shall cry, and He will say, 'Here I am.' Isaiah 58:9

When Daniel was in Babylon, he didn't take a study course to learn how to pray. He didn't need that, his people faced an existential crisis, and only God could help them. The Lord had already shown him His plans regarding His future kingdom, but the separation of God's people from the Temple in Zion meant they were missing out on what the Lord planned to do. God had declared His plans to bless his people and 'to give you a future and a hope' (Jeremiah 29:11), but they needed to go home for this to happen. And so, in response to the spiritual hunger that Babylonian paganism had generated, Daniel longed for God's presence, so he set his face to seek the Lord in heartfelt prayer. Yes, he wanted a solution to his separation. But most of all, he longed for God Himself.

> Then I set my face toward the Lord God to make request by prayer and supplications, with fasting, sackcloth, and ashes. Daniel 9:3

We see the same outpouring of heartfelt prayer from Ezra and Nehemiah. While Daniel was burdened for his people's exile to end, Nehemiah was concerned about rebuilding the Jerusalem wall, while Ezra's vision instructed him to rebuild the Temple. These were not merely architectural goals but also a desire to restore their fellowship and intimacy with their Creator. God's plan was always for deep intimacy with his people, and the children of Israel's separation through exile was never His endgame. After they learned their lessons in Babylon, He planned for them to return and rebuild the Temple. Again, God wanted to restore fellowship with His people and reopen channels of blessing between heaven and earth.

> Then you will call upon Me and go and pray to Me, and I will listen to you. And you will seek Me and find Me, when you search for Me with all your heart. Jeremiah 29:12-13

The Welsh Revival is an excellent illustration of the priority of prayer in awakening and revival. Before the Welsh Revival of 1904-1905, many people united in prayer to prepare the way for the Lord to work. In her classic work, *The Awakening in Wales*, Jesse Penn-Lewis traces what she calls 'the Hidden Springs of this mighty river of blessing' back to a groundswell of prayer. Individuals and small groups became the catalyst of what was to become a mighty gushing forth of power from on high. Just as in the time of Daniel, Ezra, and Nehemiah, the spiritual tide in Wales was out. Concern mounted about the rise of godlessness and the inability of the Church to reach the next generation. Motivated, God's people prayed. As in the early Church, heartfelt, united prayer preceded a mighty outpouring of the Holy Spirit.

> Prayer preceded the first Pentecost, and PRAYER must precede the wider outpouring of the Spirit in the last days, therefore the true members of Christ all over the world must be drawn by the Spirit within them into one accord in asking God to pour forth His Spirit according to His word. The extent of the one will govern the extent of the other, for prayer prepares the channels for the Holy Spirit to fill, and flow out through into the world. Jesse Penn-Lewis (1861-1927) [106]

There were reports of people praying for revival from faraway places like Korea and India. Home Prayer Circles were established in Melbourne, Australia, ahead of an outreach in 1901 led by RA Torrey. Ironically, although these prayer meetings produced widespread blessings, the results fell short of the widespread awakening that ignited in Wales a couple of years later.

The need for repentance

Another critical element in revivals and awakenings is that the prayers of God's people are invariably accompanied by the confession of, and dealing with, personal sin. When the Lord draws near in answer to the prayers of His people, His holy presence shines a moral light into people's hearts. When Isaiah saw the vision of the Lord in His Temple, he became aware of the Holiness of God. The Lord's presence produced an intense conviction of sin that resulted in deep repentance. Previously, Isaiah had felt comfortable speaking out to proclaim woes against various people for their failure to keep God's law. However, in God's presence, when the light of His holiness began to shine brightly, Isaiah himself came under deep conviction of sin, crying out, "woe is me"—he thought he was about to die in the light of the 'awesome crystal' of God's holiness (Ezekiel 1:22).

> So I said: "Woe is me, for I am undone! Because I am a man of unclean lips, And I dwell in the midst of a people of unclean lips; For my eyes have seen the King, The LORD of hosts." Isaiah 6:5

Before revival blessings flow to those outside the Church, God first deals with His own people. This leads to a fresh appreciation of His wonderful plan of atonement, forgiveness, and cleansing. When God's people 'humble themselves and pray,' they, in effect, open the door and invite Jesus into their situation (Revelation 3:20).

Previously, Jesus was standing at the door knocking, but prayer opens the door and grants Him access. When Jesus comes in and is given free access, everything changes.

Jesus lives in the heart of every believer, but not all Christians enjoy the blessed life God intends. If Christians focus on themselves, dominated by their human desires, Jesus will feel distant. However, when Jesus brings revival to a believer's life, His presence motivates the removal of all impediments, clearing space in their hearts for His greater presence. Writing to believers at Ephesus, the apostle Paul prayed that Jesus would dwell in their hearts through faith (Ephesians 3:17). Practically speaking, Jesus indwelt their inner being when they first trusted in Him. But He always wanted to make Himself more at home in their hearts. Previously He was a *resident* in each believer's life, but His desire was always to be the *president*.

The Holy Spirit's ministry is to convict people of 'sin, and of righteousness, and judgment' (John 16:8), in the Church as well as in the world. When believers like Isaiah began to take personal holiness seriously, God's spotlight fell on shortcomings in their lives they had not previously identified.

The deepest footprint left by the Third Great Awakening was the Holiness Movement. *The First Great Awakening* proclaimed the message of being born again, and *The Second Great Awakening* highlighted evangelism, mission, and the great commission. *The Third Great Awakening* built on these foundations and initiated a desire for personal holiness and a renewed emphasis on the need for believers to truly follow Jesus.

> Holiness is the losing of self and being clothed upon with the spirit and likeness to Jesus. [107] Andrew Murray

Holiness certainly isn't a popular topic today! Wanting to avoid the deadening effects of legalism, the modern Church has focused on God's grace and love for several generations. These are foundational New Testament truths, but as Paul pointed out nearly 2,000 years ago, God's grace should never be an excuse to justify sin or be used as permission for disobedience (Romans 6:1). Trusting in the grace of God, people who call themselves believers have justified all manner of ungodly behavior, secure in the mistaken belief that no matter how badly they have sinned, God will keep forgiving them. The flood of high-profile believers caught in immorality and the growing worldliness in the Church reflect these warped standards. It is true that God does forgive sin, but His followers are called to die to their old sinful life so that their new life in Christ may flourish.

It has become increasingly difficult to identify believers in Jesus compared to others who are thoroughly pagan. At present, there is often not much discernable difference! When so many professing Christians, leaders included, are caught up in moral scandals, communication of the Gospel suffers.

Believers who talk-the-talk but cannot walk-the-walk, play into the enemy's hands. Those who profess to follow Jesus must emulate Him. The apostle Peter explained that Jesus is holy, so too His followers are expected to be holy because He is Holy (1 Peter 1:15-16). God's people turning from their sins is not legalism. Instead, it is taking personal holiness seriously. Biblical holiness is not an option but a requirement for all believers. The Biblical word for a true believer is saint, and this word describes those who are set apart from the world to serve the Lord exclusively.

It would be a gross understatement to say that repentance and holiness aren't prevalent in many of today's Churches. However, one of the lessons of past awakenings is that before God moves in great power amongst His people, He first prepares their hearts. He did this in the lives of many of His prophets, including Isaiah and Daniel. God's preparation of individuals for revival through prayer and personal repentance has featured in all the awakenings and revivals in history. This pattern emerged in the Welsh Revival of 1904-1905, the Hebrides Revival of 1949-1952, and the Canadian Revival of the early 1970s, to name just a few.

One of the lesser-known accounts from the Hebrides revival (1949-1952) is how the Lord prepared His people's hearts before He stepped down in revival power in these islands off the west coast of Scotland. The believers stunted spiritual lives were evident, manifested by falling church attendances. Young people had deserted the Church, which motivated leaders to call their people to pray. However, after some months of fervent prayer, the leaders became convicted of their need to get right with God. Only then would He have the freedom to move in their churches and communities. One of the leaders was impressed by a question the Psalmist asked: 'Who may ascend into the hill of the LORD? Or who may stand in His holy place? (Psalms 24:3). These same church leaders who had been praying for revival and the salvation of others felt convicted of their own sin. With those crucial convictions addressed, the heavens opened, and revival fell.

> Brethren," he said, "We have been praying for months for revival, waiting before God, but I would like to ask you now: ARE OUR HEARTS CLEAN? IS THE HEART PURE?" In response to this searching challenge they fell upon their knees in confession, and rededication, and again began to travail in prayer, even more earnestly. An hour later, three of them were lying prostrate upon the floor—they had PRAYED UNTIL THEY WERE EXHAUSTED! By five o'clock revival had come. The barn was suddenly filled with the Glory of God, and the power of God that was let loose in that barn shook the whole community of Lewis. Rev Owen Murphy [108]

Once again, the precursor to revival was passionate, united prayer by a small group of believers. Owen Murphy's book, When God Stepped Down from Heaven, proves that a prayer meeting can change history. Released, the Holy Spirit was free to descend on the Churches; believers were strengthened, souls were saved, and Hebrides communities transformed.

Consecration: creating space for God to work

Following the poverty of spirit that motivates prayer and repentance, the next step in the pattern of awakening is consecration. This is when people fully and willfully dedicate themselves to the Lord, giving Him all authority to act in their lives. As Isaiah's life story unfolds, we see that after his conviction of sin and God's wonderful provision of forgiveness and cleansing, the Lord stakes a claim on the prophet's life. The incredible revelation of God's grace and forgiveness leads to God challenging Isaiah: 'Who will go for us'? (Isaiah 6:8). Now in a place of close fellowship with the Lord, the issue of serving and obedience came into focus.

Centuries later, the apostle Paul writing to the Romans, stated that based on all Jesus has done for us, the believer's only reasonable response ought to be total consecration. Just as the Old Testament Temple was to be holy and set apart for God's exclusive use, so too the believer is called to be set apart for the Master's use.

> I beseech you therefore, brethren, by the mercies of God, that you present your bodies a living sacrifice, holy, acceptable to God, which is your reasonable service. And do not be conformed to this world, but be transformed by the renewing of your mind, that you may prove what is that good and acceptable and perfect will of God. Romans 12:1-2

Such has been the pattern of awakenings throughout history. Following prayer and repentance, the focus rests solely on the Lord's agenda: His salvation for all.

After Jesus' death and resurrection, His disciples willingly consecrated themselves to serve Him as He directed. They counted it a privilege to work for Jesus no matter the cost. A flame of holy love burned in their hearts, and nothing was beyond expressing appreciation for all Jesus had done for them.

In previous generations, young men and women volunteered in their thousands to serve the Lord sacrificially in foreign missions, usually at high personal cost. They esteemed it a privilege to serve the Lord. Today, by contrast, Churches count themselves successful if they can retain the young men and women who come up through their children's and youth programs—a further reason we urgently need an awakening today.

The fire falls

In both the Old and New Testaments, the pouring out of God's presence and power confirmed a believer's or Church's consecration to Him. At the dedication of Solomon's Temple, after its cleansing and dedication to God's exclusive use, 'fire came down from heaven and consumed the burnt offering sacrifices, and the glory of the LORD filled the temple' (2 Chronicles 7:1). The Shekinah glory of the Lord was such that the priests could not enter because 'the glory of the LORD had filled the LORD'S house (2 Chronicles 7:2). So too, when the Lord Jesus consecrated Himself to His Father's will at baptism in the River Jordan, the Holy Spirit descended and anointed Him for His mission (Luke 3:22). Announcing the Kingdom of God, Jesus issued His call to discipleship, a heart consecration to His will. It was those fully consecrated to His service, obedient to His will, that met in the upper room to wait for the Promise of the Father (Luke 24:49).

It was Jesus Himself who promised the gift of the Holy Spirit. As the Spirit fell on the believers gathered in the Upper Room, visible tongues of fire appeared—He had ignited a fire of Holy Love in the hearts of His followers. Only then could His disciples obey His commands, known as the royal law of love (James 2:8). Finally, Jesus' name was glorified, and believers were brought into the fullness of the Holy Spirit, as He had promised.

> You never have to advertise a fire. Everyone comes running when there's a fire. Likewise, if your church is on fire, you will not have to advertise it. The community will already know it.
> Leonard Ravenhill

Nine

THE CHURCH THAT JESUS BUILT

> The age of miracles is not past. Jesus changed unresisting water into wine, but the Holy Ghost transfigures the sinful soul bristling with antagonisms, transforming depravity to purity by the mighty alchemy of love. The power to effect such revolutions in character constitutes the standing miracle of Christianity. Daniel Steele, *Love Enthroned*

What is a Christian?

In an episode of the TV series The Crown, Queen Elizabeth invited the American evangelist, Dr. Billy Graham, to speak at her private chapel. The message Dr. Graham preached on this occasion was both insightful and inspired. To the titled head of the Church of England, his message was, 'What is a Christian?' Dr. Graham explained that a true Christian in the Biblical sense is someone in whom Jesus Christ lives. We need to be reminded of this great Biblical truth today. A genuine Christian is someone who has been born again by the operation of the Holy Spirit and in whom Jesus resides and with whom the believer is acquainted by personal experience. The apostle Paul defined the Christian life as, 'Christ in you, the hope of Glory' (Colossians 1:27). A person cannot become a Christian through self-effort or religious observance. It is God's work from beginning to end. Culture changes, and society is always in a state of flux, but some things remain constant. It remains that we become a Christian by the regenerating work of the Holy Spirit, the beneficiary of grace through faith. When Jesus said, "Receive the Holy Spirit" (John 20:21), He used the same words employed in Genesis when God breathed into Adam the breath of life (Genesis 2:7). Jesus didn't come to establish a new religion but to restore the life of God to our fallen humanity.

> Being a Christian is more than just an instantaneous conversion—it is a daily process whereby you grow to be more and more like Christ. Billy Graham

Dr Graham's choice of topics at that time was of strategic importance because the word *Christian* has come to mean different things to different people. In some cases, it has nothing to do with following Jesus or emulating the pattern of the Church that Jesus built. There are, for example, those who see Christianity in merely cultural terms and are committed to *cultural Christianity*. Such people identify with the cultural trappings of Christianity but know little or nothing of its heart. A 2018 poll of 15 European nations reported that 91% of respondents were baptized as Christians, [109] 81% were raised as Christians, and 71% identified themselves as Christians. However, the reality is that despite these impressive statistics, only a tiny percentage of people in Western Europe *attend* Church, live out their faith, and put it into practice. The inescapable conclusion is that many want to identify with the ideals and benefits of Christianity without taking the teaching of Jesus seriously.

Commentators more qualified than I have addressed the decline in Church attendance and Western culture's increased rejection of the Christian faith. The research indicates that attendance at public worship has declined dramatically over the past few generations. However, I believe that in many cases, the people who have stopped attending haven't necessarily rejected Jesus or His teachings. Instead, they have become disillusioned with how the contemporary church expresses the Christian faith. People in general still admire the Sermon on the Mount and the golden rule taught by Jesus. They are, however, turned off by the hypocrisy of those who profess such high ideals but offer no authentic expression. Putting it as simply as possible, the West has primarily rejected 'church' while many believers still aspire to the teaching of Jesus and the ideals of the Christian faith.

> Man was so engineered by God that the presence of the Creator within the creature is indispensable to His humanity. Major Ian Thomas

For the light of the Gospel to shine brightly in the present darkness, there must first be a more authentic expression of the Christian faith, one that fully embodies the life of God. Second, there must be a return to the New Testament Church, the Church that Jesus built. I am not advocating a new denomination or movement, but rather the growth to full maturity of the existing Church. The need is of such urgency that we may need another reformation. The first reformation restored the New Testament teaching of justification and salvation to the Church. Examining the Church that Jesus built will lead to the rediscovery of Biblical sanctification—the believer's growth to maturity through faith in Jesus.

When Jesus came as the Savior of the world, He invested in a small group of people who became His disciples. He invited them to spend time with Him, follow His teachings, and witness His faith in action as He taught spiritual truth. Jesus' central focus wasn't a one-hour church service each Sunday but on a unique relationship with His followers. Mark's Gospel teaches us that Jesus called His disciples to be with Him (Mark 3:14). They were no longer people who had willfully gone astray but sheep that had returned home to their heavenly Shepherd (1 Peter 2:25). Their message was that eternal life is knowing the one true God personally and intimately (John 17:3). The capstone to Jesus' discipleship training came when His followers witnessed His death and resurrection and received the outpouring of the Holy Spirit on the day of Pentecost.

Initially, only 120 of His followers met to pray, but God used this small group to launch a peaceful revolution destined to change the world forever. In contrast to the contemporary Church, the Church that Jesus built was unstoppable because it experienced 'the power of God unto salvation' (Romans 1:16). Jesus had already transformed their lives, and they knew He would change the lives of others when they came face to face with the truth.

Instead of rejecting Jesus out of hand, Western society needs a more authentic expression of His life, teaching, and transforming power. That is why we urgently need another spiritual awakening in our generation. Today, more than ever, we need His forgiveness, hope, and love to permeate our hearts, lives, and especially our society. Once the traditional church's ornate religious façade and cultural packaging are removed, a profound and very precious reality remains. However, it is in grave danger of being lost. Those who follow Jesus must mature past spiritual infancy and become the victorious, fruitful people Jesus called them to be.

Banks train their employees to detect counterfeit banknotes by thoroughly examining the authentic, legally minted originals. So too, we need to focus on the heaven-sent original instead of the artificial counterfeit. Instead of describing those manifestations of the Christian faith that fall below the New Testament standard, we should reflect on the Church that Jesus built. Here are just some of the critical features of the New Testament Church.

- The Church that Jesus built crowned Him as their Lord
- The Church that Jesus built followed Him
- The Church that Jesus built had Jesus in its midst
- The Church that Jesus built was victorious

The Church's one foundation

The Church that Jesus built crowned Him as their Lord. His Lordship was its central message. As the Gospel accounts unfolded, we learned the first disciples were eyewitnesses of Jesus' death and His resurrection. Having beaten death and accomplished what no one else in history had achieved, Jesus was "declared to be the Son of God with power according to the Spirit of holiness, by the resurrection from the dead" (Romans 1:4). As well as motivated by His divine love and sacrifice, those who followed Jesus gladly submitted to His Lordship, knowing that He and He alone was the way to eternal life. The salvation that Jesus delivered was not only about the objective fact of His resurrection but also the subjective reality that demonstrated He was alive and living in their hearts.

His divine presence was transformative, giving life to those who were spiritually dead. He gave sight to those who had been spiritually blind and deposited love in the hearts of people previously motivated by selfishness. His divine love produced obedience in the lives of people who had rebelled against the reign of God. With Jesus in their hearts, they could live victoriously and fruitfully as He alone gave them the deep desires of their hearts (Psalm 37:4).

> Therefore, let all the house of Israel know assuredly that God has made this Jesus, whom you crucified, both Lord and Christ.
> Acts 2:36

At Caesarea Philippi, the apostle Peter made the declaration of faith that caused Jesus to respond: "It is on *this* rock that I will build *my* Church." It is against this scriptural pattern that all other expressions of Church must be measured. The purpose of the Church that Jesus built was to implement the heavenly plans of the Father, who gave planet earth His Son as the instrument of salvation. Therefore, it is absurd to declare that 'Jesus is Lord' without obeying His directions.

Jesus' teaching at Caesarea Philippi was a stroke of genius from the most outstanding teacher our world has known. But, of course, we would expect nothing less from the Son of God! Jesus and His disciples lived in a world ruled by the Roman Caesars, who believed they were demigods. Here, at Caesarea Philippi, Philip the Tetrarch built a marble shrine dedicated to the worship of Augustus Caesar, a site used for pagan worship for centuries. Amongst its attractions was a cave known as the Gates of Hades, dedicated to the worship of Pan. It was here that Jesus declared He was the Son of God and that He alone was to be worshipped above the Roman emperor and all the so-called gods of the pagan pantheon.

On their way to Caesarea Philippi, Jesus asked His disciples a rhetorical question: "who do men say that I am?" Not satisfied with their responses, He repeated the question that everyone on planet earth must answer at some time. "Who do *you* say that I am?" Peter stepped forward and made his momentous declaration, "You are the Christ, the Son of the living God" (Matthew 16:16). As soon as Peter verbalized this profound statement of faith, Jesus commended him, declaring that *this* Truth was the foundation on which he would build *His* Church. Moreover, Peter's verbalization of Jesus' Lordship earned His complete approval, "Blessed are you, Simon Bar-Jonah, for flesh and blood has not revealed this to you, but My Father who is in heaven (Matthew 16:17). Thus, Jesus Christ alone is the foundation of His Church, a church comprised of people who, by simple faith, embrace His Lordship, follow Him and receive their life from Him.

> A day must come in our lives as definite as the day of our conversion, when we give up all right to ourselves and submit to the absolute Lordship of Jesus Christ. From that day we are no longer our own masters but only stewards. Not until the Lordship of Christ in our hearts is a settled thing can the Spirit really operate effectively in us. Watchman Nee [110]

The challenge for today's leaders is to scrap the man-made traditions that caused millions to lose faith in the Church. When the leadership starts walking in the pure light of New Testament teaching, the Church will again become the magnet that revolutionized the world 2000 years ago. Encouraged by leadership to embrace Jesus' Lordship, believers will have no option but to live in sync with His ways. The old saying is true: 'If Jesus isn't Lord of all, He really isn't Lord at all!' There is nothing we can do to earn God's favor when we are born again. However, once we have become Jesus' followers, we can only walk with Him in obedience to His will.

Once Jesus' Lordship is accepted, His Church must take His instructions seriously enough to obey them. Failure to bite the bullet and take a stand for New Testament truth now will only accelerate the Western Church's slide into oblivion—
God help us!

Jesus commanded His disciples to make disciples

Churches today are frequently undecided whether to focus on evangelism and winning new converts or devote themselves to the nurture of existing members. When believers take Jesus' Lordship seriously, then *both* become important. The Great Commission recorded in Matthew 28:18-20 shows us that 'make disciples' is a *command*. 'Making disciples' was the command given by Jesus, and *going*, *baptizing*, and *teaching* were the three participles outlining the activities that support this imperative. These other things, though important, were not to be their priority in themselves and were only a support to the main task. To know the truth about Jesus and not want to share it with others doesn't make sense. New believers desire to share their faith from the very beginning of their Christian walk. The Church that Jesus built produced disciples who followed Him and were committed to making converts and disciples.

The Christian life is counter-intuitive to human reason as it requires the surrender of our *natural* life to receive a new, *supernatural* life from heaven. Discipleship or following Jesus is not merely about the transfer of information but rather the communication of LIFE. Humanly speaking, it seems unlikely that anyone would willingly and voluntarily surrender their human autonomy and take their orders from someone else. That is why our secular age has insisted on choosing its own plan of salvation independent of God. There is, however, a divine paradox, a profound mystery in play. The message of God's love resonates deeply in the depths of our humanity so that people of all ages have been motivated to surrender their autonomy to God to receive a brand-new heavenly life here on earth.

Jesus' commanded His disciples to be filled with the Holy Spirit

Paul's teaching regarding the Christian walk emphasized the need to be filled with the Holy Spirit. But unfortunately, the converse of this teaching means that it is possible for a believer not to be filled. Instead of the Holy Spirit ruling and reigning in a believer's life, their human nature dominates. It is usually only when the new believer realizes their absolute inability to live the Christian life through human effort that they seek to be filled and empowered by the Holy Spirit.

> And do not be drunk with wine, in which is dissipation; but be filled with the Spirit, Ephesians 5:18

Sometimes people are filled with the Holy Spirit at conversion, and indeed, that is what happens in times of revival and awakening. For others, it occurs after conversion resulting from the believer's growth in faith as they learn to receive what God has promised to give. Whatever your theological background or tradition, this instruction through Jesus' servant Paul is in the imperative mood; it is not an option but a command. The order to be filled with the Holy Spirit is just as binding as the negative command not to be drunk with wine. These are moral choices that sincere followers of Jesus must take seriously.

Following Paul's instruction to be filled with the Holy Spirit is the most ethereal and heavenly teaching on human relationships, enriched by Jesus' presence and sanctified by holy love. These teachings of the need for love in all human relationships provided the foundational fabric of Western society for centuries. These values urgently need to be restored to reverse the moral and spiritual decline.

> This, of course, is what it means to be filled with the Holy Spirit—to allow the Holy Spirit to occupy the whole of your personality with the adequacy of Christ. Major Ian Thomas
> *The Saving Life of Christ*

Being filled with the Holy Spirit enables the believer to rise above their human selfishness and be filled with the Holy love of God. The first followers of Jesus surrendered that innate selfishness that has been the scourge of humanity to embrace divine love, the most extraordinary power in the universe. Their love of Jesus motivated them to follow Him in love and trustful obedience.

- Divine love is foundational to our relationships with other believers (Ephesians 5:2, Ephesians 4:1-6,

- Divine love is foundational to our marriage relationships (Ephesians 5:22-33)

- Divine love is foundational to all parent/child relationships (Ephesians 6:1-3)

- Divine love is necessary for harmony in the workplace (Ephesians 6:5-9

Jesus commanded His disciples to be Holy

The word *holy* is used throughout the Bible to describe God's character and moral excellence. The Lord said to his redeemed people, "you shall be holy; for I am holy" (Leviticus 11:44). His command was not optional but a part of His overall plan for His people. The apostle Peter made it abundantly clear that this was still binding in God's New Testament covenant of grace. Holiness is not so much a legal requirement but a heart choice. Born-again believers receive a new nature to serve the Lord, and every believer's heart cries out to be more like Him. It is a universal law that we take on the nature of whatever we worship. If the object of our worship is a pagan idol, the Bible says, 'Those who make them are like them; so is everyone who trusts in them.' Those who follow Jesus are to emulate Him. Jesus taught that unless a person surrenders their autonomy and selfish sinfulness, he *cannot* be His disciple (John 14:26-27).

The apostle Paul described two ways to live the Christian life. The first is to walk according to the Spirit, and the second is through human effort. Unfortunately, these alternatives are opposites. The desire for holiness motivates the believer to choose the will of God in daily life. The other way, which Paul called the works of the flesh, produces frustration and failure.

> Do not be deceived, God is not mocked; for whatever a man sows, that he will also reap. For he who sows to his flesh will of the flesh reap corruption, but he who sows to the Spirit will of the Spirit reap everlasting life. Galatians 6:7-8

The Church that Jesus built followed HIM

At Caesarea Philippi, Jesus demanded a 180-degree turn from allegiance to the kingdoms of man to follow Him. Genuine saving faith not only changes our way of thinking but our trajectory in life and, ultimately, our eternal destiny. When people follow Him, it is because He deserves to be the Lord of their life forever. For this to happen, those who seek to follow Jesus must first surrender their autonomy and give up their petty little kingdoms to embrace the Kingdom of God.

> Then Jesus said to His disciples, "If anyone desires to come after Me, let him deny himself, and take up his cross, and follow Me. For whoever desires to save his life will lose it, but whoever loses his life for My sake will find it." Matthew 16:24-25

Jesus didn't only die on the Cross to deliver a not guilty verdict for His followers. His plan from the beginning was that they would transform from the inside out. The idea that people would call themselves followers of Jesus and live a life no different from their pagan neighbors is unthinkable.

When the apostle Peter identified Jesus as the coming Messiah, He would fulfill all of God's promises to save humanity from itself. Therefore, seekers of Jesus must surrender their lives to Him, take up their spiritual cross, and follow in His footsteps. Such is life for those whose hearts have changed through the New Birth.

> The greatest marvels of the Gospel scheme are not only in the facts of Christ's earthly life, death, and resurrection, but in the wondrous transformation wrought by the Holy Spirit in the soul of the believer who apprehends the exceeding greatness of his power to us-ward who believe. Daniel Steele [111]

When an individual recognizes their sin and asks Jesus for forgiveness, God can perform a great miracle in their life. The heart that sincerely repents is changed and regenerated through the operation of the Holy Spirit. The apostle Paul stated that when a person receives Jesus as their Savior, it is as though they have become a brand-new creation. While today's science community seeks to explain the origins of the existing physical universe, the Lord is already working on an entirely new project. The apostle Paul stated: If anyone is in Christ, he is a new creation; old things have passed away; behold, all things have become new (2 Corinthians 5:17).

The Cross has been the universal emblem of Christianity throughout history. This profoundly simple symbol magnificently encapsulates the Gospel message in all its glory. The Cross portrays Jesus' personal experience in this world and marks the path that his disciples must follow. To follow Jesus requires that we walk the same spiritual pathway that He walked. Not all Jesus' followers will walk the path of martyrdom, but every disciple must surrender and consecrate his life to God.

> When Christ calls a man, he bids him come and die. Dietrich Bonhoeffer [112]

The ordinance of baptism powerfully displays the spiritual implications of surrendering one's life to the Lord to live a completely new life. When someone publicly identified as a follower of Jesus in the early Church, they underwent baptism. Different groups interpret baptism differently, but it is still universally practiced by believers. The mode of baptism may be open to interpretation, but the truth it conveys is not. Only those who surrender their lives can follow Jesus, and only those who follow Him belong to His Church. The true Church of Jesus Christ comprises those who recognize Him as their Lord and have chosen to follow Him through the Cross. There is no other way.

The apostle Peter illustrated the necessity of this radical spiritual revolution when, on the one hand, he called Jesus 'Lord' and then proceeded to instruct Him on how he would run things. On the other hand, when Peter made his declaration that Jesus was indeed the Jewish messiah (Matthew 16:16), the Lord commended him that he had got this right. It was then that Jesus intimated to the disciples that His pathway would lead to Jerusalem and the Cross, but Peter didn't like the idea: "Peter took him aside and began to rebuke him. "Never, Lord!" he said. 'This shall never happen to you!'" (Matthew 16:22 NIV). Nevertheless, Jesus' pathway led Him to the Cross and resurrection. Before Peter could follow Jesus, he had to set aside his agendas and follow Jesus.

Throughout history, there have been those who called themselves Christians but have been unwilling to follow Jesus in His proscribed way. Instead, they have sought to reinterpret the terms and conditions of what it means to follow Him. They want the blessings but are not prepared to pay what has been called the cost of discipleship. Thus, Jesus rebuked Peter and all those seeking to emulate Peter's Cross-denying compromise throughout the ages. Peter later became an esteemed apostle, but his initial attempts to turn Jesus from the way of the Cross earned the sternest possible rebuke: "Get behind Me, Satan! You are an offense to me, for you are not mindful of the things of God, but the things of men" (Matthew 16:23).

It is imperative in these times of post-modern, post-truth confusion that believers clearly understand their identity and mission. Jesus made it clear that these things are simply non-negotiable. When today's Church wakes up and acknowledges that JESUS is their Lord, and His word is final, then they will follow only Him and Him alone. When they do this, they will also discover the same thing that the pagan Romans learned to their regret; that the Church that Jesus built is impregnable because the divine Presence indwells it.

Jesus amid His Church

The Church that Jesus built was not a religious club for the benefit of its members and guests. Genuine followers of Jesus Christ are not concerned with a mere religious observance or following a code of ethics, but instead being the Body of Christ in whom their risen Savior lives and abides. In the Old Testament, God dwelt in a temple made of stone. In the New Testament, He lived in the hearts and lives of 'living stones' that collectively formed a spiritual temple. The Bible teaches that 'the Most High no longer dwells in temples made with hands, (Acts 7:48), but only in a spiritual temple that He alone can build. The Church that Jesus built is a spiritual temple comprising of Jesus' followers in whom He lives.

> We who believe are carefully joined together, becoming a holy temple for the Lord. Ephesians 2:21 NLT

Jesus explained that although He was going away, He would not abandon them and leave them as spiritual orphans (John 14:18). The whole object of His plan of salvation was to bring people into fellowship with Himself, and this didn't end with the ascension of Jesus to heaven. When He poured the Holy Spirit into the hearts surrendered to Him, God's plan took on a whole new meaning. Everything changed from then on—their focus was on knowing Jesus and making Him known.

From the beginning, the Church's activities revolved around their relationship with Jesus and their devotion to Him. Thus, the same chapter that recorded the outpouring of the Holy Spirit on the day of Pentecost also gives a precious little cameo picture of the Holy Spirit-inspired activities. These activities built their faith, increased their spiritual intimacy with Jesus, and enriched their walk with Him.

> And they continued steadfastly in the apostles' doctrine and fellowship, in the breaking of bread, and in prayers. Acts 2:42

The above scripture referred to the four primary spiritual practices of the early Church. These are the same core activities by which today's Church can grow in faith and personally experience Jesus.

- Believers sought to know Jesus through the Word of God.
- They talked with Jesus in prayer.
- They experienced Jesus' life through fellowship with other believers.
- They enjoyed communion with Jesus through the Lord's Supper and worship.

The Church Jesus built was a victorious Church

Built on the foundation of faith in the Son of God, the Church that Jesus built was unstoppable. With Jesus in its midst, no power in the universe could prevent His disciples from fulfilling their mission. The triumvirate of evil known as *the world, the flesh*, and the *devil*, were powerless to stop the counterrevolution of light against the spiritual darkness of the First Century world. Jesus exposed pagan deceptions as they surrendered to the Light of the World. Satan's power and his dark kingdom could not match the almighty power of God. When the Lord of heaven chooses to act, no force in heaven or earth can stop Him. Jesus' arrival ignited the most incredible reset in history. When His light shines brightly in seasons of revival and awakening, the darkness will never extinguish it.

When Jesus died on the Cross and rose again, He won a mighty victory over the world, the flesh, and the devil, and He delegated His mighty power to His Church. He planned that she, too, could walk in the victory that He had already won. Having laid down their lives to follow Jesus, they had already gained a victory over the world. With their sins forgiven and Jesus indwelling, every child of God can rise above the limitations of their fallen nature, giving them victory over their flesh. With their sins forgiven, the devil can no longer accuse and harass God's dear children.

The Church that Jesus established understood that evangelism is primarily a spiritual battle. Although there must be an appeal to people's minds and wills, man's rebellion against God is fundamentally a spiritual issue. According to pagan tradition, the cave of Pan at Caesarea Philippi featured a pit known as the gates of Hades, said to have no bottom, reaching down into the earth's bowels, the underworld. Adjacent to this pagan site, Jesus made His momentous declaration that the Church that He built would stand firm against the powers of darkness. The kingdom of God was ready to plunder the realm of evil. The light of the Gospel was poised to plunder Satan's kingdom, to set people free from ignorance and bondage forever.

> And I also say to you that you are Peter, and on this rock, I will build My church, and the gates of Hades shall not prevail against it. Matthew 16:18

We are indebted to the book of Revelation and the apostle John's behind-the-scenes insight into the cosmic struggle that has dominated world history to the present day. John records a voice in heaven saying, "Now salvation, and strength, and the kingdom of our God, and the power of His Christ have come, for the accuser of our brethren, who accused them before our God day and night, has been cast down (Revelation 12:10). Leaving aside any discussion of the prophetic application of this declaration, we embrace the glorious truth that the Lord has given His Church victory over Satan and all his powers of darkness. God's word declares that because salvation and strength and the kingdom of God have come, every child of God can overcome their spiritual enemy. We read that "they overcame him by the blood of the Lamb and by the word of their testimony, and they did not love their lives to the death (Revelation 12:11).

Victory over their spiritual enemy has been the privilege of every child of God throughout the Church's history. It was true in the early Church as it was in the time of Martin Luther (1483-1546), whose faith in God's word triggered the Reformation. So, it is also true today in these last days as the Lord prepares His Church for the final consummation of the ages:

> *Though devils all the world should fill,*
> *All eager to devour us.*
> *We tremble not, we fear no ill,*
> *They shall not overpower us.*
> *This world's prince may still*
> *Scowl fierce as he will,*
> *He can harm us none,*
> *He's judged; the deed is done;*
> *One little word can fell him.*
> *—Martin Luther* [113]

Ten

MAKING THE MAIN THING THE *MAIN* THING!!

> Love is the end of confusion.
> Bishop Festo Kivengere (1919-1988)

I once saw a plaque in a gift shop with the inscription:

'Life takes you to unexpected places. Love brings you home.'

This striking statement made me stop and think. While not always true of romantic love, it is true of God's love. The desire to love and be loved is embedded deep within our inner being; it is the foundational necessity in all our human and Divine relationships. God's love is the vital ingredient missing in every secular and pagan heart. Frantically searching for love-substitutes, the material world is more than ready for the Real Thing, perhaps more than ever before. Pure unadulterated love drew Jesus to the Cross, bearing the sins that we could not carry ourselves. Now, the Cross of Jesus is a beacon of light and hope shining brightly throughout the present darkness to light the path that will lead us home.

The choice is now yours. You can close this book and vainly hope the world might become a better place. Or you can join thousands of sincere believers around the globe, daily on their knees, crying out to God for His next great awakening. If God's love doesn't bring the West home, chaos and strife will indeed become our legacy.

> Only the Gospel of the Lord Jesus Christ has the power to turn the tide!

Until Jesus came, the pre-Christian pagan world had no concept of the self-giving divine love that He revealed as the greatest power in the universe. The impact of the Gospel lay in the fact that divine love fulfills every human aspiration for something better—that is, for peace, joy, love, freedom, and especially eternal life. God created us in His image, so death seems foreign, cruel, and unfair. Jesus' self-sacrificial death on the Cross, followed by His glorious resurrection, changed everything.

For this reason, despite fierce opposition, the Gospel message spread throughout the first-century world. Jesus' divine love was so revolutionary and different from all previous understandings of human relationships that they had to coin a new term to describe it. The word used in the Gospels was *agape*, the supreme self-giving love that puts others' welfare before our own. Jesus Christ manifested this divine love, which His followers emulated. In English, we only have one word to describe intense love, but the Greeks had several different words for the various kinds of love. They used *philos* to describe emotional love and *eros* for physical and romantic love. The love that Jesus both taught and demonstrated was a spiritual self-giving love. He told of it Himself when He said: "Greater love has no one than this, than to lay down one's life for his friends" (John 15:13).

The Cross of Calvary reminds us that Jesus Christ, the Son of God, surrendered His life for others as an act of love. Jesus' self-sacrificial agape love is the measure of divine love. The entire Bible can be paraphrased with the familiar scripture: "For God so loved the world that He gave His only begotten Son, that whoever believes in Him should not perish but have everlasting life" (John 3:16).

Because of our innate desire, deeply embedded in our DNA, to love and be loved, God ordained Jesus' love to be the beacon to lead His people home to Himself. Love is so powerful that it can soften the hardest of hearts. It is the only power capable of freeing us from our selfish sinfulness. In the early church days, people like the apostle Paul who had previously rejected Him, responded to the Gospel of love to become His followers. God's love can soften the hardest heart. Through God's transforming miracle of grace and love, the Church was born, and the world was to be changed forever. The message of the first-century Church was that Jesus had conquered death and was both Lord and Christ so that through Him, everyone on earth could conquer death and overcome the limitations of their base humanity. This understanding that God loves us and wants us to invest in other peoples' welfare provides Western civilization's spiritual, philosophical, and cultural foundations.

> Love, hope, fear, faith—these make humanity; these are its sign and note and character. Robert Browning (1812-1889)

There is an old saying that love makes the world go around, and there is a good deal of truth in this. Just as the planets orbit the sun perfectly, we were designed to revolve around our Creator and heavenly Father. Love is the only glue that can cement our relationships; with God and others. When we enter a love relationship with God, our lives become ordered, empowered, and fruitful. Our response to His love reconciles heaven and earth, enabling us to experience perfect peace with God and enjoy His love that is greater than we can even imagine. Once reconciled to God, our ongoing relationship with Jesus transforms us from the inside and becomes the first step to changing our world for the better. So, it is true that even though life takes us to unexpected places, divine love brings us home.

> He that enters the Holiest finds there the God of love. Andrew Murray (1828-1917) [114]

All you need is love!

Having rejected God, the source of love, the West has abandoned its spiritual life and direction. It has lost the cohesive glue that once held it together. It has been more than 50 years since the Beatles sang: All You Need is Love. However, for these young men, their desire for love was only aspirational in that they couldn't even get along with each other. Nothing had changed; the same is evidenced throughout history and is just as accurate today. Jesus alone is the source of divine love. Our only experience of agape love is in fellowship with Him. LOVE is the fruit of the Spirit and the supernatural outcome of living in a relationship with Jesus.

In these days of post-modern, post-truth confusion, God's divine love is like a laser beam leading us home to our heavenly Father. Just as in Jesus' parable of the Prodigal Son, it was when the son had squandered his inheritance and was destitute that he experienced first-hand the emptiness and cruelty of life. It was then that he chose to return home to his father and become the recipient of his father's love.

The love that every human being on earth desires exists in fellowship with Jesus Christ. He is the source of divine love because love is of God. The apostle John was one of Jesus' original twelve disciples and the apostle of love. John taught: Beloved, let us love one another, for love is of God; and everyone who loves is born of God and knows God (1 John 4:7).

Having witnessed Jesus' teaching and healing ministry, and then later His death and resurrection, those first followers of Jesus were willing to not only live their life following Jesus but also, if necessary, to die a martyr's death. They understood that the Gospel held the very meaning of life as it resonated with our need to love and be loved.

> Behold what manner of love the Father has bestowed on us, that we should be called children of God! Therefore the world does not know us, because it did not know Him. 1 John 3:1

People need to know that there is still hope for humanity in a world that is increasingly alienated, unfriendly and hostile, emotionally crippled, morally bankrupt, toxic, and deeply divided. There is an answer to all the inhuman obscenities that typify Western society. Protesting the darkness accomplishes little or nothing. What people need is to turn to the light of the Gospel. Only then will they discover that there is a God who loves them. However, for the simple, unadorned Gospel to pierce the present darkness, the need of the hour is for the followers of Jesus to make room in their hearts and lives for Him so that He can shine forth from their lives. That has been the pattern of awakenings throughout history, and the need is greater today than at any other time in history. For this to happen, God's people must lay aside all impediments and, if necessary, remove the cultural wrappings that can hide the glory of the Cross and allow the Lord to rekindle the fire of sacred love in our hearts. Only then will the main thing once more become the MAIN thing.

Heaven's divine love is the main thing

The fruit of the Spirit

Because God is the source, we can only experience this eternal divine love by living in fellowship with Him. Using the metaphor of a grapevine, the apostle Paul explained to the believers in Galatia that just as the branch belonging to a grapevine produces grapes, so too it is the believer's relationship to Jesus that delivers divine love. Love is the fruit of the Spirit. Just as the branch attached to a grapevine grows fruit, Jesus will produce fruit in the life of someone who is in an active, living relationship with Him. That is not only a spiritual principle but also a guarantee from God. It is a law of nature and a law of the Holy Spirit. Our growth to maturity as believers isn't automatic but results from 'abiding' or remaining in a vital fellowship with Jesus. The fruit of the believer's relationship to God will always be divine love in all its various manifestations.

> But the fruit of the Spirit is love, joy, peace, longsuffering, kindness, goodness, faithfulness, gentleness, self-control. Against such, there is no law. Galatians 5:22-23

No matter how hard we try or how high our aspirations to experience divine love apart from God may be, human effort can never produce the fruit of the Spirit. Believers only experience God's love by His life manifested within them. Paul explained in the most precise way that because God is the source of all love, only He can produce this highly desirable fruit that is indispensable to our human wellbeing. The fruit of the Spirit is the visible, measurable outcome of His influence on our lives as we live in fellowship with Him. This fruit that the Holy Spirit produces in a life yielded to him is love in all its many-colored expressions. Just as light passing through a prism displays a variety of colors, so too does divine love manifest itself in various ways through the context of our day-to-day experiences.

G. Campbell Morgan (1863-1945), a noted Bible expositor of a previous generation, made the point that the word *fruit* is singular in the original Greek language, meaning there is only *one* fruit of the Spirit. The fruit of the Spirit is *love*. The other so-called fruits listed in the Galatians passage are simply the manifestations of love in the various areas of our life.

The Fruit of the Spirit is ... LOVE!

Joy is Love's *Consciousness*
Peace is Love's *Confidence*
Longsuffering is Love's *Habit*
Kindness is Love's *Activity*
Goodness is Love's *Quality*
Faithfulness is Love's *Quantity*
Meekness is Love's *Tone*
Temperance is Love's *Victory*!

Jesus didn't die on the Cross to create ineffective, spiritually impotent, and confused Christians. Instead, he intended that His followers would grow to full maturity and be filled and empowered by the Holy Spirit. Jesus' first disciples understood this and turned the world upside down. The experiences of the early Church will happen again when his people finally wake up to the present challenges and grow up and mature! Only then will believers fulfill the destiny for which they were created. The Church will become God's glorious dwelling place that He ordained. When individuals wake up and grow up, God's people will enjoy God's fulness by making the main thing the MAIN thing, and protest against the present darkness will have begun.

The inadequacy of human effort

In the context of Christian maturity, Paul explained in his first epistle to the Corinthians that as well as being the measure of an individual believer's spiritual growth, *love* is also the measure of a Church. The manifestation of love, or its lack, is the critical indicator of whether it genuinely follows Jesus. Paul explained in a very confronting way that it is impossible to produce the fruit of the Spirit through self-effort. This fact hasn't stopped people down through the ages trying to do the work of God through human endeavor. The apostle Paul's asked: 'Are you so foolish? Having begun in the Spirit, are you now being made perfect by the flesh?' (Galatians 3:3).

> Alas, how little has Christ's Church proved that it has its birth from the God of love, that it owes its all to Him who loved us, gave us the new commandment of love, and asked us to prove our love to Him by bestowing it on our brethren. Andrew Murray [115]

The plain truth is that it is possible to pray, share the Gospel, study the Bible and run Church programs without God's help at all. Paul explained that many of the highly prized attributes in the Church community are worthless if they are not motivated by divine love. 1 Corinthians 13 is generally known as the love chapter, and here Paul explained that as far as the Church's life in any age is concerned, love must be the main thing. Apart from divine love, all Church activities are ineffective and a waste of energy; they can even be counterproductive.

> Though I speak with the tongues of men and of angels, but have not love, I have become sounding brass or a clanging cymbal. And though I have the gift of prophecy, and understand all mysteries and all knowledge, and though I have all faith, so that I could remove mountains, but have not love, I am nothing. And though I bestow all my goods to feed the poor, and though I give my body to be burned, but have not love, it profits me nothing. 1 Corinthians 13:1-3

This challenging passage of Scripture reminds us of what *should* be the focus of the Church. If love isn't central, it negates the impact of all our other activities. If Paul were addressing the Church today, I am sure he would make it clear that whatever our tradition, love is more important than:

- *The tongues of men*—oratory and skillfully used words
- *The tongues of angels* – a heavenly prayer language—the gift of tongues
- *The gift of prophecy*—the proclamation and declaration of God's Word
- *Understand all mysteries and knowledge*—academic attainment
- *Faith to move mountains*—the faith that makes things happen
- *Bestow my goods to feed the poor*—Social justice and welfare programs
- *Give my body to be burned*—self-sacrifice and service

Paul says that *none* of these things that are so highly esteemed in our Church culture today mean anything if they aren't motivated by a heart full of love. Apart from the fire of holy love, there is nothing of the divine in our life, Christian walk, or service. Apart from God's agape love, our actions, attitudes, and communications will only be like all the other background noise around us in our world today. Christian ministry is only transformative when it is motivated by *love*. If the Church is to effectively communicate the Gospel to a lost and confused world, it must once more radiate the light of God's love.

To once more shine forth the divine love of God, the Church must grow to full spiritual maturity. This may mean another reformation that is just as impacting as that which restored the Biblical doctrine of *justification*. Today's Church must rediscover the doctrine of *sanctification* by faith and how believers may grow to full maturity in Christ. Divine love is not about virtue signaling and creating a favorable media profile but rather the demonstration of self-giving love that puts others first.

> What does love look like? It has the hands to help others. It has the feet to hasten to the poor and needy. It has eyes to see misery and want. It has the ears to hear the sighs and sorrows of men. That is what love looks like. Augustine of Hippo (A.D. 353-430)

The greatest reset in history was a revolution of love. It was about bringing down the strongholds of selfishness and self-aggrandizement and replacing them with the divine love of the kingdom of heaven. The love that every human being on earth desires is only found in fellowship with Jesus Christ. He alone is the source of divine love because 'love is of God', and this reality has powerfully impacted hearts and lives from the first century to the present day. The appeal of secularism over the past 50 years is it promises all the benefits of liberal democracy without the moral price tag. Sadly, this delusion overlooked that, apart from God, man is fatally flawed and his own worst enemy. The West's rejection of God has facilitated a return of pre-Christian paganism with its myriad social ills. This rejection is the sole cause of the serious malaise that people now see and feel.

The apostle of Love

The apostle John was one of Jesus' original twelve disciples and was known as the apostle of love. John was one of Jesus' inner circle, who later was the author of five books of the New Testament. Together with his brother James, he became one of Jesus' first disciples after He invited them to follow Him. Together with Peter and James, John later became a part of Jesus' inner circle, being with Him when Jairus' daughter was raised from the dead as well as being with Him on the mount of transfiguration.

Tradition holds that John was sentenced to death in a boiling vat of oil. Yet he emerged unharmed from the experience. Later, John was exiled to the island of Patmos, where he penned the book of the Revelation, dying in Ephesus at an old age around 98 A.D. In his commentary on Galatians 6:10, Jerome (c.342-420A.D.) tells us that in extreme old age John was so frail that his students had to carry him to Church. Only able to mutter a few words, John would repeatedly say, "Little children, love one another." Annoyed that John kept repeating himself, his students and others in Church asked why he kept repeating the same thing over and over. John replied, "Because it is the Lord's commandment and if it alone is kept, it is sufficient." John recorded these thoughts in his first epistle when he wrote: Beloved, let us love one another, for love is of God; and everyone who loves is born of God and knows God (1 John 4:7).

Having witnessed Jesus' teaching and healing ministry, and then later His death and resurrection, John, as well as the other disciples, were willing to not only live their life following Jesus but also, if necessary, to die a martyr's death. They understood that the Gospel held the very meaning of life as it resonated with the need to love and be loved that embeds our human DNA.

In a world that is increasingly alienated, unfriendly and hostile, emotionally crippled, morally bankrupt, toxic, and deeply divided, people need to know that there *is* still hope for the human race. There is an answer to all the inhuman obscenities that typify Western society. Protesting the darkness accomplishes little or nothing. What people need is to turn to the light of the Gospel. Only then will they discover for themselves that there *is* a God who loves them. However, for the simple, unadorned Gospel to pierce the present darkness, the need of the hour is for the followers of Jesus to make room in their hearts and lives for Him so that He can shine forth from their lives. That has been the pattern of awakenings throughout history, and the need is greater today than at any other time in history. For this to happen, God's people must lay aside all impediments and, if necessary, remove the cultural wrappings that can hide the glory of the Cross and allow the Lord to rekindle the fire of sacred love in our hearts. Only then will the *main* thing once more become the MAIN thing. Heaven's divine love is the main thing.

> Behold what manner of love the Father has bestowed on us, that we should be called children of God! Therefore the world does not know us, because it did not know Him. 1 John 3:1

The triumph of light over darkness

Divine *love* was the preeminent attribute in the life and ministry of Jesus. Most profoundly, Jesus taught His first disciples that the *one thing* that identifies His genuine followers is divine, holy, self-sacrificing *LOVE*. This love can't be manufactured through human self-effort and is the fruit of the Spirit. Love supernaturally manifests in a person's life when Jesus transforms them through their relationship with Him. So, I am convinced of the need for today's Church to make the main thing, LOVE, the *main* thing!

> A new commandment I give to you, that you love one another; as I have loved you, that you also love one another. "By this, all will know that you are My disciples, if you have love for one another." John 13:34-35

Like light, *love* is self-authenticating and universally recognized as of great value. Love is the beacon that will lead us home to God because it is such a rarity in this dark world. Following Jesus as a disciple involves sacrificing our own life to invest in the welfare and happiness of others. The supreme example of God's agape love was seen in the Cross of Jesus when he sacrificed His own life so that others might live. This love is the opposite of 'survival of the fittest' and the dog-eat-dog paganism of our age. It goes against the instincts of our selfish sinfulness.

> Greater love has no one than this, than to lay down one's life for his friends. Jesus, John 15:13

The outpouring of divine love ignited the Gospel revolution that resulted in the greatest reset in history. The Gospel's impact was such that believers planted churches in all the important population centers of the Roman Empire within the first generation. This is a testimony to the superiority of light over darkness. This same pattern emerged in the various awakenings of history when the light of the Gospel once more shone brightly, and people saw Jesus for who He was, as the Light of the World.

> The history of God's intercourse with men is the chronicle of his love. This is the only history which will outlive itself, and escape the conflagration which will burn up the world and all the works therein. Daniel Steele (1824-1914) [116]

Tertullian (ca. 160–220 A.D.) was a citizen of Carthage in North Africa, a part of the Roman Empire, and was later known as the Father of Latin Theology. When he became a follower of Jesus, Tertullian used his formal secularist education to apply reason and logic to show that the Christian life is vastly superior to paganism. Tertullian was raised in a pagan family and educated in Latin grammar, rhetoric, and philosophy. These disciplines were needed by those aspiring to be lawyers or Roman civil servants at that time. In middle age, Tertullian chose to follow Jesus and became an influential church leader. Because of his academic background, he would leverage his intellect and education, together with his personal experience of Jesus, to become a formidable theologian. The Apostle Peter taught that Christians should be able to explain their faith and give a reason (Greek: *apologia*) for what they believe and why they believe it (1 Peter 3:15). Tertullian mastered this ability at a very effective level.

Because of his unique gifting and qualifications, Tertullian explained the benefits of following Jesus to a pagan society opposed to the Gospel. His reasoning is critical today as we reflect on our own culture that has replaced the worship of God with recycled pre-Christian paganism. In Tertullian's

Apology, destined to become a Christian classic, Tertullian stated that Christianity offered a superior quality of life based on integrity and love.

For Tertullian, *love* was the ultimate apologetic. He attacked his day's pagan beliefs as superstitious and immoral with exceptional literary and intellectual skill.

He then asked his readers to consider the contrast between the Christian and pagan ways of life, comparisons that would be obvious to any thinking, educated, fair-minded person.

In individual life and society in general, paganism was an empty, futile dead-end. However, to those born and raised in the moral sewer of paganism, the higher moral life of the early Christian community had strong appeal. Divine love stood out clearly in their dark world and softened their hard pagan hearts; it overcame their base instincts biased towards selfishness and sensual pleasure.

> But it is mainly the deeds of a love so noble that lead many to put a brand upon us. See, they say, how they love one another, for themselves are animated by mutual hatred; how they are ready even to die for one another, for they themselves will sooner put to death. And they are wroth with us, too, because we call each other brethren; Tertullian [117] (c.155–220 A.D.)

The persecution of the Christian community by the Roman Emperors contrasted the light and darkness. Diocletian's ridiculous pretensions to be a god and the moral bankruptcy of Roman society prepared people's hearts to accept the truth and opened their eyes to the light. In a dog-eat-dog world, love always stands out. The testimony of these brave martyrs had a profound and lasting effect as the light of the Gospel dawned on the pagan darkness of the Roman Empire. The West was poised to enter a whole new phase of its history.

> The blood of the martyrs is the seed of the church. Tertullian (A.D. 155-220) [118]

From its humble beginnings in the Roman province of Judaea, the light of the Gospel shone brightly throughout the pagan darkness of the Roman Empire. Ultimately, the fire of God's love and its heavenly light conquered the entrenched paganism of Rome. As a result, Christianity became the official religion of the empire. The light did shine in the darkness, and the darkness could not comprehend or overcome it.

Only *love* produces spiritual offspring!

Alongside the Bible's teaching of the sovereignty of God is the great mystery that believers are co-workers with Him (1 Corinthians 3:9). In His great wisdom, He has chosen to work on planet earth through His Church, the body of Christ, to interface with a lost world and bring others home to Himself. Although the Lord chooses to work through His followers, the blessings of the Christian life are not bestowed on believers automatically—but only in response to their faith. Human cooperation is required to receive each of the promised blessings, to the call to abide in Christ, be filled with the Spirit, and take up the armor of God. Each of these beautiful provisions are received by faith. So too, the Lord works on earth in response to intercession and prayer. Intercession lies deep in the heart of God and is an essential part of His plan of salvation.

Intercession is one of Jesus' chief activities as the great high priest. As a practical expression of His love, we read that: 'He always lives to make intercession for them' (Hebrews 7:25). Both Jesus and His disciples were devoted to intercession because intercessory *prayer* is a practical outworking of the believer's faith in God. Filled and empowered by divine love, Jesus' Church was motivated to both pray and actively manifest the love of God.

When people become followers of Jesus, they invest in the welfare of others. Jesus' disciples understand that somehow, somewhere, someone must accept the responsibility for the eternal destiny of another human being. The most loving and practical way to help someone that is blind to the love of God is to intercede for them; praying that they will be born again of the Spirit. Motivated by divine love, believers bring their friends, relatives, and acquaintances to the throne of God in prayer. In times of revival and awakening, crowds get swept into the Kingdom of God through the prayers of God's people.

We see this spiritual principle illustrated in the teaching of the apostle John. In his first epistle, John referenced spiritual *infants, young men,* and *spiritual fathers* (I John 2:12-14). Spiritual *young men* have grown in their faith and have the spiritual strength to stand against the powers of darkness. Likewise, spiritual *fathers* have grown in spiritual maturity to where they are willing and able to accept responsibility for the welfare of others.

> Like natural children, spiritual children don't simply appear out of nowhere. Instead, spiritual children are the offspring of those who care and love enough to intercede for the salvation of others

In a particularly insightful passage of scripture, the apostle Paul explained how the planting of the Church in Galatia was the direct result of his intercession. Just as a mother goes through physical labor to birth a child, Paul interceded in a spiritual process to birth salvation for those in Galatia. We have a vivid insight into this spiritual birth process because of their stunted growth. Paul had to begin the process of spiritual travail, birth pangs, and intercession all over again.

My little children, for whom I labor in birth again until Christ is formed in you. Galatians 4:19

It was God's design that earthly children would be conceived and born as an expression of the mutual love of their parents. The apostle Paul explained that human marriage is a great mystery and the love between a husband and wife is a picture of the love of Jesus Christ for His Church (Ephesians 5:32). This helps explain the divine love that God pours into believers' hearts to motivate them to intercede for fellow human beings. Spiritual offspring arise from these expressions of practical divine love. If we neglect intercessory prayer, spiritual reproduction will suffer.

The Holy fire of love-constraining

If there is to be a turning of the tide against the present darkness, a fire of holy love must first be re-kindled in the Church of Jesus Christ. Before there is an awakening in our world, there must first be a revival in the Church.

This must begin with the re-affirming of Jesus Christ as Lord, followed by a passionate desire to follow *Him*. For those who have left their first love and sincere devotion to Jesus is no longer paramount, there will need to be serious adjustments. May the Lord give us a fresh revelation of His glory that surpasses all others and cause us to seek Him above all else. Only then will He be able to kindle a fresh fire of holy love in their hearts and those of their fellow believers.

Turning the Tide in the West

> If there is to be a turning of the tide against the present darkness, a fire of holy love must first be re-kindled in the Church of Jesus Christ. Before there is an awakening in our world, there must first be a revival in the Church.

There are still billions of people on planet earth still in darkness and have never even heard that there is a God who loves them deeply. The sacrifice that Jesus made for us demands something more from His people than passive indifference. Indifference is an offense to the Lord and leaves the heart lukewarm and empty. Just as in Moses' life, when people see the divine light and power burning brightly in a humble thorn bush, they will stop and take notice—and awakening will already have begun.

I conclude with the words of a hymn by Charles Wesley (1707-1788). The terms and spelling may be archaic, but the message is as relevant as this morning's news blog. Charles, and his better-known brother John, had an impeccable religious pedigree. They were the sons of a clergyman, educated at Oxford, and ordained ministers in the Church of England. However, an intense need for something more motivated them to seek after a close personal experience of God. Charles and his famous brother John found what they were looking for in Jesus. The fire of the Gospel ignited both their hearts. The Wesley brothers joined George Whitfield and others to become a part of a band of brothers that God used mightily in the First Great Awakening. Charles' hymn expresses the divine holy love overflowing from a grateful heart. It has been the means of blessing to many thousands and perhaps even millions of people right up to the present day. May this also be the prayer of our own hearts in these dark and challenging days.

O Thou Who Camest from Above,

O Thou Who camest from above,
The pure celestial fire to impart,
Kindle a flame of sacred love
Upon the mean altar of my heart.

There let it for Thy glory burn
With inextinguishable blaze,
And trembling to its source return,
In humble prayer and fervent praise.

Turning the Tide in the West

*Jesus, confirm my heart's desire
To work and speak and think for Thee;
Still let me guard the holy fire,
And still stir up Thy gift in me.*

*Ready for all Thy perfect will,
My acts of faith and love repeat,
Till death Thy endless mercies seal,
And make my sacrifice complete.*

Charles Wesley

Turning the Tide in the West

EPILOGUE

> Now may the God of hope fill you with all joy and peace in believing, that you may abound in hope by the power of the Holy Spirit —Romans 15:13

The restoration of hope

Hope is in short supply and is desperately needed in these days when many see the future only in apocalyptic terms. At the time of writing, Russia had recently launched its invasion of Ukraine with the widespread recognition that the West had failed to prevent this catastrophe.

Even sincere followers of Jesus need reminding that God is the source of all hope, and with it, the expectation that He will act on our behalf for good. The secularist belief in man's abilities offers no reason for hope. In contrast, faith and hope in God, open endless possibilities.

The Living Bible translates Psalm 42:11 and its declaration, 'hope in God' as: *'Expect God to act.'* Hope flows from our faith in God. *Faith* is the inward union of the soul with Jesus and *Hope* is the consequence of that faith. Hope enables the believer to confidently expect that God will act on their behalf. That is why the apostle Paul was able to say with confidence, 'Hope will not lead to disappointment' (Romans 5:5 TLB).

> Faith is the inward union of the soul with Jesus and Hope is the consequence of that faith.

For the follower of Jesus, the best is yet to come because we live in hope. This confident expectation that God will act on our behalf encourages us to call on the Lord and expect Him to send revival in our day. He has done it before, and He can do it again.

The three great pursuits of the Christian life are not "miracles, power, and gifts"; they are **faith**, **hope**, and **love**. David Guzik [119]

When Jesus' followers get their eyes off the present darkness and start to call on the name of the Lord, their hope will be restored, and God will begin to move in a new and powerful way. Today, hope is in short supply and will remain so until God's people humble themselves and *pray*!

Where do I start?

If you have read thus far and recognized your country's urgent need for a mighty move of God in these days, allow me to offer a few practical steps for your consideration. In the chapter 'Calling on the name of the Lord,' I suggested you should call on the Lord for His help. If this is the first time you have taken God seriously, you must begin by joining His team, getting behind His program, and receive His Holy Spirit into your heart by faith. Perhaps your family has associated with a particular denomination, and you believe in God but have never known Him personally. I encourage you to turn from following the secularist values described in this book and consciously decide to follow Jesus. Ask Him to forgive your sins and make you a child of God. (For a more comprehensive explanation of this amazing new life, check the Billy Graham Evangelistic Association's webpage, the section 'My Peace with God.')[120]

> But as many as received Him, to them He gave the right to become children of God, to those who believe in His name.
> John 1:12

For those who already follow Jesus as their Lord and Savior, I recommend setting aside time each day to read the Bible and pray. Then ask Him to bring revival to your own heart by inviting Him in—to do a new and deeper work.

Someone asked the English evangelist Gypsy Smith (1860-1947), how to experience revival; "Go home, lock yourself in a closet. Kneel in the middle of the floor and draw a chalk circle around yourself. Ask God to send revival inside that chalk circle. When God answers your prayers, then revival will come!" [121]

Also, if you appear to be a lone voice crying out for Him to move in a new way, pray that He will draw another person of like mind.

Great power is unleashed when a believer prays, but this effect is multiplied when believers pray together.

Then, once you have a prayer partner, you can pray together for a third member, thereby initiating a prayer triplet. God has ushered in His mightiest works in the past when just a few humble, passionate believers pray together. Do not be paralyzed by feelings of helplessness. The doors of heaven await your knock.

Pray together for the Lord to bless your Church leaders, as well as your fellow believers in your local congregation. Intercede for your community. Ask Him to step down and move in the same way He has done so many times in the past.

Finally, for those who desire more of God, I encourage you to visit my website www.desdaniels.com. There you will find additional resources to assist and hopefully inspire you in your quest for revival.

ENDNOTES

INTRODUCTION THE GAME HAS RADICALLY CHANGED
[1] Kenneth Scott Latourette. Chapter 9: *The Shock of Augmented Revolution, A.D. 1750-1875 Christianity Through the Ages*

CHAPTER ONE THE GREATEST RESET IN HISTORY
[2] J.H. Merle d'Aubigne. *The Reformation in England*. Volume I P.144 Banner of Truth
[3] Jennifer Oriel, *Russian Revolution: Communist barbarians led us to genocide*, The Australian, October 8, 2017
[4] Galatians 4:4
[5] *Logos*. Philosophy and Theology, Encyclopedia Britannica
[6] *Logos*. Philosophy and Theology, Encyclopedia Britannica
[7] Conybeare and Howson. *The Life and Epistles of St. Paul*. P.3
[8] Ken Curtis, PH.D. *The Spread of the Early Church*, christianity.com
[9] Major W. Ian Thomas, *RELIGIOUS OR CHRISTIAN?*, From the foreword of *Classic Christianity* by Bob George, Eugene: Harvest House Publishers. ©1989.
[10] I have not been able to find the source of this quote that is repeated all over the internet. The closest I have come to a peer-reviewed article was *Malcolm Muggeridge*, Conservapedia.com
[11] Matthew 2:16
[12] *Rome The Power and the Glory*, Discovery Channel. This figure was also estimated by English Historian Sharon Turner
[13] *The Tenth Persecution, Under Diocletian, A.D. 303*. Biblestudytools.com
[14] Manning Clarke, *A History of Australia*
[15] BBC Website, *Christianity In Britain*, Constantine and Augustine. Last updated April 27, 2011

CHAPTER TWO HEAVEN'S PEACE PLAN
[16] *Wild brawl between pedestrian and cyclist at Prahran caught on film*, 9News, 7:36am, September 14, 2018
[17] 1 Peter 1:12
[18] *The Christmas Truce*, Snopes Fact Check
[19] In 1960 Dr Billy Graham said: "World leaders have asked me, "What is

wrong with the world? Why can we not solve our problems?" Each time I have replied, "It is impossible for you to understand what is happening in the world until you understand that this is spiritual warfare." Billy Graham: *The Problem with Our World*, September 2, 2013,

[20] Isaiah 53:3
[21] Isaiah 53:5
[22] Charles Wesley, *And can it be?*
[23] Cecil Alexander, *There is a green hill far away*
[24] Philippians 4:7
[25] William Barclay, THE INCLUSIVE CHURCH (Romans 15:7-13), William Barclay's Daily Study Bible
[26] William Barclay, William Barclay's Daily Study Bible, Romans 15 THE INCLUSIVE CHURCH (Romans 15:7-13) iii (a)
[27] Romans 2:15, Romans 1:19
[28] Jeremiah 31:33
[29] Sir Isaac Newton, *General Scholium*, The General Scholium to Isaac Newton's Principia Mathematica, Isaac-Newton.org

CHAPTER THREE THE NEED FOR REVIVAL TODAY

[30] National Secular Society, *What is Secularism?* https://www.secularism.org.uk/what-is-secularism.html
[31] William Floyd, The Humanist (Vol. 2, 1942, p. 2): Floyd was one of the signers of the Humanist Manifesto 1
[32] Although quoted widely on the internet, I was not able to track the source of this quotation. One website, The Minds Journal, appears to offer itself as the source although this is not clear
    https://themindsjournal.com/i-think-everybody-should-get-rich/
[34] A.N. Wilson, *The Book of the People*, 2016
[35] President Lincoln, Illinois Republican State Convention, Springfield, Illinois June 16, 1858
[36] Robert Skidelsky, *Is western civilization in terminal decline?* The Guardian 17 November 2015
[37] *Lord Denning*, Number Three Equity Court, Legal Present, and the musings of a country lawyer, Friday May 26, 2017, https://number3equitycourt.blogspot.com/2017/05/lord-denning.html
[38] David Matthew, *I Saw the Welsh Revival*, Chapter 1 Reminiscences of the Great Welsh Revival.

[39] Jonathan Sandys & Wallace Henley, *God and Churchill*. SPCK, P.163
[40] Deuteronomy 30:16
[41] Romans 6:23
[42] D. James Kennedy, *Why the Ten Commandments Matter*.
[43] Os Guinness, *The Dust of Death*, P.38
[44] *Reports of Mark Twain's quip about his death are greatly misquoted...* June 02, 2018, ThisDayinQuotes.com
[45] D.A. Carson, *How Long, O Lord?*
[46] Janet Albrechtsen, *We are funding our own demise*, The Australian 21 June 2018
[47] Greg Sheriden, *Is God dead? The West has much to lose in banishing Christianity*. The Australian, August 26, 2017
[48] World History Encyclopedia, *The Sack of Rome 410 CE*, "With a little help from inside the city, the Salarian gate was opened, and Alaric and his army of 40,000 marched into the city."
[49] Dr. Martyn Lloyd-Jones. *The Christian Warfare*. P.27 Banner of Truth
[50] Victor Hugo, *Les Miserables*, Chapter XI, Christus Nos Liberavit
[51] Luke 15:17
[52] Philip D. Jensen, *Prodigal World, how we abandoned God and suffered the consequences*, Matthias Media. 2003
[53] Francis Thompson, *The Hound of Heaven*,

CHAPTER FOUR THE LIGHT IS STILL SHINING

[54] Martyn Lloyd-Jones, *The Cross*, p.60, Crossway Books 1986
[55] Andrew Bolt, *Civilisation in flames*, (Australian) Daily Telegraph. April 18, 2019
[56] Josh Hafner, *The cross still stands and votives remained lit. Signs of hope out of the Notre Dame Cathedral fire*, USA Today, April 16, 2019
[57] Alex Lasker, *Powerful image shows cross shining through wreckage at Notre Dame Cathedral*, AOL April 16 2019-07-29
[58] Guy Millière, *The Burning of Notre Dame and the Destruction of Christian Europe*, Gatestone Institute April 22, 2019
[59] Roy Hession *We Would see Jesus*, p31
[60] FB Meyer, The Trinity of Temptation, P.126 *The Soul's Ascent*, Horace Marshall and Son, 1901
[61] John 19:20
[62] John 19:38-39

CHAPTER FIVE THE AWAKENINGS OF THE PAST

[64] James Packer, *Your Father Loves You*, Harold Shaw Publishers, 1986, page for May 30.

[64] I haven't been able to trace the source of this quotation, but it is widely quoted on the internet and was also mentioned by J. Edwin Orr, in his article *Prayer and Revival*,

[64] Greg Laurie, *It's Time for Another Jesus Revolution*, Charisma Magazine, 9/12/2018

[65] Robert J. Morgan, *The Sixth Great Awakening: America's Only Hope*, Huffington Post, June 11, 2013

[66] C.G. Finney *The Role of Prayer in Spiritual Awakening*

[67] Jonathan Edwards. *A Faithful Narrative of the Surprising Work of God*

[68] Rev. Owen Murphy *When God Stepped Down from Heaven*

[69] Roy Hession (1908-1992) *We Would See Jesus*, Preface P.2

[70] 1 Timothy 1:15

[71] William Ngenda was a leader in the East African revival and was also a colleague of Roy Hession author of *The Calvary Road*.

[72] Autobiography of Charles Finney quoted by John Greenfield *Power from on High*. 1927

[73] Dan Graves, *John Wesley's Heart Strangely Warmed*, Church History, Timeline 1701-1800, Christianity.com

[74] Frank McLynn, *Crime and Punishment in Eighteenth Century England* Routledge. P.4

[75] Robert J. Morgan. Huffington Post June 11, 2013 *The Sixth Great Awakening: America's Only Hope*

[76] MEN OF FAITH- the Methodist faith of the martyrs, Tolpuddle Methodist Church- website-http://www.tolpuddlemethodists.org.uk

CHAPTER SIX RE-DIGGING THE ANCIENT WELLS

[77] P.27 *BE AUTHENTIC* Warren Wiersbe. David C Cook Second Edition 2010

[78] Martyn Lloyd-Jones *Joy Unspeakable* P.401

[79] Baptist History Homepage, *JOHN SUTCLIFF, "THE PRAYER CALL OF 1784"* http://baptisthistoryhomepage.com/1784.cl.british.prayer.html

[80] *The Prayer Call of 1784* Michael G Haykin historian with the Andrew Fuller Center, Southern Baptist Theological Seminary.

[81] Population of India, Population of the world. Livepopulation.com

[82] *Shaping the Australian Baptist Movement*. Dr. Ken Manley.

[83] J. Edwin Orr, *Prayer and Revival*
[84] J. Edwin Orr, *Prayer and Revival*
[85] *What Is the Summary of The Second Great Awakening?* Reference.com
[86] *In the Wake of the Second Great Awakening*, Christianity Today
[87] *In the Wake of the Second Great Awakening*, Christianity Today
[88] Dan Graves, *Jeremy Lanphier Led Prayer Revival*, Christianity.com
[89] Jesse Penn Lewis THE AWAKENING IN WALES P.14-15

CHAPTER SEVEN CALLING ON THE NAME OF THE LORD

[90] Source Professor Barth's student: Jan Milič Lochman, "Towards an ecumenical account of hope," The ecumenical review 31, no. 1 (January 1979): 18 (13-30) = Midstream18, no. 1 (January 1979): 30 (24-34).
[91] Genesis 3:15
[92] Ephesians 2:12
[93] Ephesians 6:10
[94] Ephesians 6:11-12, 14-17
[95] 2 Corinthians 10:3-4
[96] Charles G. Finney *Revival Lectures*, P.49
[97] Jim Cymbala, *Fresh Wind, Fresh Fire*.
[98] David E. Gardiner, *The Miracle of Dunkirk: 70 years on*, Christians Together 21 August 2019, https://www.christianstogether.net
[99] David E Gardiner, *The Miracle of Dunkirk 70 years on*
[100] Parker, WG, *A Historical link with 1941-World War II*, cited by the Wikipedia reference to this hymn
[101] Words attributed to Admiral Yamamoto 1970 film *Tora, Tora Tora,*

CHAPTER EIGHT THE BIBLICAL PATTERN OF AWAKENING

[102] Roy Hession, *My Calvary Road* P.13 Chapter One "*Revival-The Bottom Falling Out*" CLC 2011
[103] William Ngenda was a leader in the East African revival and a colleague of Roy Hession, author of *The Calvary Road*.
[104] David McCusland, *Oswald Chambers: Abandoned to God*, (1993) Discovery House, P.84
[105] David McCusland, *Oswald Chambers: Abandoned to God*, (1993) Discovery House, P.85
[106] Jesse Penn-Lewis, *The Awakening in Wales and some of the Hidden Springs*, Chapter 1, p.12

[107] Andrew Murray *The Holiest of All*, P.448
[108] Rev Owen Murphy, *When God Stepped Down from Heaven*

CHAPTER NINE THE CHURCH THAT JESUS BUILT
[109] *Being Christian in Western Europe*. Pew Forum, May 29, 2018
[110] Watchman Nee, *The Normal Christian Life*, P. 97
[111] Daniel Steele *Love Enthroned* P.2 CCEL
[112] Dietrich Bonhoeffer, *The Cost of Discipleship* (London: SCM Press, 1948/2001), 44.
[113] Martin Luther, *A mighty fortress is our God*

CHAPTER TEN MAKING THE MAIN THING THE *MAIN* THING!
[114] Andrew Murray, *The Holiest of All*, P. 518
[115] Andrew Murray, *The Holiest of All*, P. 518
[116] Daniel Steele *Love Enthroned* P.2
[117] Tertullian *Apology* Chapter 39 Tertullian. (1885). (S. Thelwall, Tran.) *The Ante-Nicene Fathers, Volume III: Latin Christianity: Its Founder, Tertullian* (p. 55). Buffalo, NY: Christian Literature Company.
[118] This is the more common rendition of *"The oftener we are mown down by you, the more in number we grow; the blood of Christians is seed."* Tertullian. (1885). The Apology. (S. Thelwall, Tran.) *The Ante-Nicene Fathers, Volume III: Latin Christianity: Its Founder, Tertullian* (p. 55). Buffalo, NY: Christian Literature Company.
[119] David Guzik, 1 Corinthians 13 Commentary, Precept Austin website
[120] Billy Graham Evangelistic Association, *My Peace with God*, https://lp.billygraham.org/my-peace-with-god/
Additionally there is a dedicated website, that offers the same information: https://peacewithgod.net/mobile/
[121] Deborah S. Macomber, *Gipsy Smith*, Berean Bible Heritage Church, https://bereanbibleheritage.org/extraordinary/smith_rodney.php

www.ingramcontent.com/pod-product-compliance
Lightning Source LLC
Chambersburg PA
CBHW051437290426
44109CB00016B/1596